CHAPTER 1

Introduction

"Children are not things to be molded, but are people to be unfolded."

~ Jess Lair

"Like tiny seeds with potent power to push through tough ground and become mighty trees, we hold innate reserves of unimaginable strength. We are resilient."

~ Catherine DeVrye

What is life? Biologically speaking, life is anything that grows and eventually dies, i.e., ceases to proliferate and be cognizant. A human being is a higher form of life having a well-developed brain that regulates all life activities and can explain the meaning, i.e., the purpose of life.

Human Life is the features of birth and existence

CHILDHOOD MIND AND EDUCATION

Reframe and overcome the Challenges

Childhood Mind and Education Challenges, Strategic action points for Parents, Teachers, Society, policymakers to
mitigate. Building Child's Foundation, Achieve Goals, Fulfilling life, and Happiness

DHARMESWAR DAS

TABLE OF CONTENTS

that evolves through reproduction, metabolism, growth, and numerous processes. In general, terms, when one asks what life is, it means what exactly is the "meaning of life."

There exist seven aspects of the life process:

1. Physical health consists of the performance of all body's biological functions coordinating smoothly with mental health.

2. Mind and mindset with a huge amount of drive, energy, and functionality to consistently grow to achieve the desires.

3. Fulfilments of family and Relationships with others.

4. Education, Work, and Career trajectory and Prosperity.

5. Wealth and earning Satisfaction.

6. Spiritual Wellness and ability to absorb philosophy behind life.

7. Mental strength and mindset to perform and behave.

The meaning of life is the ideals imposed upon it and demanded to execute. Natural intuitions determine the meaning of life, and these intuitions resonate throughout life, giving it its purpose.

Life is made meaningful with its values in human minds and is subject to change at times and conditions. It is, therefore, said that "Many men, many minds."

Many phases in a person's life are described in various terms by different people. Life is a journey. There are different stages of life with the progression of age; each stage of life impacts the other. One school of thought explains that different life stages intersect with six life domains. These are prenatal/infancy, early childhood, school age, transition to adulthood, and adulthood. Some others again explain that the average human life span falls into nine stages: prenatal development, infancy and toddlerhood, early childhood, middle childhood, adolescence, early adulthood, middle adulthood, late adulthood, and old age leading to dying and death.

Together, the stages of life impact and influence the trajectory of life, i.e., the path a person's life journey takes. One's analysis of life trajectory can help in finding out what has helped or hindered in the past and what may be influencing the way forward. For instance, the higher a person's expectations, the person will always seek opportunities. This will provide more experiences to the person and help them achieve their goals. Different phases of life and their understanding explaining the life course and trajectory is the science and philosophy of life and its purpose.

A person's life changes with the changing time and growth of the body and mind in different phases from birth to adulthood in the process of aging. The body's morphological development and physiological changes occur due to hormonal actions produced by the commands of various genes and their interactions with environmental factors. The development of the human body and mind continues throughout life.

All the characteristics of the body forms and functions, behaviour, and emotions change with the progression of time and age. The brain of humans controls the execution of these changes throughout life. However, the process of learning and understanding the self and others of a person are associated with different ages, and this is a continuing challenge in one's life. It requires in-depth observation and understanding.

The stages of life give a point of reference to

observe various developmental signs and attain maturity. This provides support whenever needed along the course of their life. The transitions that are taking place in the body, mind, psychology, and expression and behaviour in or between any of these stages are very critical to the individual. It is a challenging job for the individual and the people they are associated with within their family or society.

Therefore, growing and navigating from one stage to another, from childhood to adolescence, with the accompanying physical, hormonal, emotional, mental, and social changes, is a challenging task for the individual in the progression of their lives and those around them.

Understanding the different stages and challenges of life therein helps to recognize the signs of concern through every age and stage of life along with their needs. This understanding of life revolves around fulfilling the basic physical requirements and the required mindsets. To create good connections with others with love and belongingness and the development of personal and cultural identities and strengths, a support system needs to be developed to help others in distress.

It is a fact that the physical and mental traits coupled with the mindset of the person interplay or interact with each other. This interplay is responsible for producing the quality and sustainability of outcomes fulfilling the basic philosophy of life. Families and communities can be most resilient when people can support each other's needs well through every age and stage of their life process. Ultimately, the meaning of life is to live life meaningfully and with peace and happiness, which are achievable only by working together.

CHAPTER 2

Phases of human life

"It's not the years in your life that count.
It's the life in your years."

~ Abraham Lincoln

The maximum possible human life span is about 130 years. The major stages of the human lifecycle are infancy, from birth to one year of age; toddler, during ages two to the end of early childhood at three years of age, childhood from four years of age to eight years; puberty, the period from nine years of age till thirteen years, i.e., the beginning of adolescence. The older adolescence starts from fourteen years of age to eighteen years. The adulthood period starts from nineteen years of age till the end of life. The Middle age of human life is the period of adulthood that stretches from thirty-one to fifty. The old age extends from fifty-one to the end of life.

Early childhood is comprised of the period of infancy and the toddler years. The remaining part of childhood is the period from ages four through eight, during which the children enter school and their educational life begins.

As a general concept, a person's life has four phases, viz., childhood, youth, adulthood, and old age. Different kinds of evolving challenges are encountered during these phases in terms of physical, physiological, mental, and psychological growth and development. Phases of life, in general, refer to the biological classification of the changes that occur in the body due to aging. However, the upcoming generations sometimes tend to change traditional views and challenge many aspects of life processes. They try to redefine the process by crossing the psychological norms and barriers hitherto laid down by their predecessors. Indeed, this psychological and analytical behaviour is also an evolving process of eugenics in an approach towards bettering themselves to adapt to the fast-changing scenario of the world environment.

Eyal N. Danona, a life coach, founder of the Ignite

Advisory Group, and author of "The Principle of 18: Getting the Most Out of Every Stage in Your Life," suggested a new description of the life process to explain the different phases of life. This classification of life phases is based on life's mental and psychological journey. Accordingly, the five main phases of life have been designed as an alternative life system based on the activities of life and living of the person developed by interacting with inner intuition, instinct, and desire. The phases are described as (1) Dreamer stage, (2) Explorer stage, (3) Builder stage, (4) Mentor stage, and (5) Giver stage.

This description of a life system has been articulated to enable a person to live a happier, satisfied, and meaningful life in the present minimizing regrets of being unable to do something in the past. Thereby it has an inherent capacity that can overcome the problem of the unhappiness of not achieving a person's desire at a certain stage of life. Besides that, this description has been considered to have the required ingredients to realize the potential of five interconnected stages from the Dreamer to the Giver stage. Each stage of life consists of a person 18 years of age; therefore, this description is called the "Principle of 18".

The Dreamer stage, from birth to 18 years of age, focuses on the process that is the key to creating a vision with a serious expectation of becoming a reality.

The Explorer stage of life is from 18 to 36 years of age. This stage is committed to a serious exploration and effort that leads to the areas where one will excel and be the most passionate. In this stage, one tries to come out of their comfort zone, take risks as an explorer, and achieve the goal at any cost, meeting the challenges come what may.

The Builder stage is from 36 years to 54 years of age. In this, one tries to establish the foundation of experience, determination, and self-awareness, fully leveraging on own talents of the person. In this stage, one will jump on opportunities doubling their efforts and sustaining the intensity of the Builder phase keeping the mind open for all avenues and options to achieve results.

During the Mentor Stage, between the ages of 54 and 72, individuals take on the role of mentor, utilizing their experiences to guide and support others. This stage is highly valuable as individuals possess the skills and knowledge to handle challenges, overcome obstacles, and develop important qualities such as perseverance, perspective, and courage.

In the Giver Stage, from ages 72 to 90, one can finally fully enjoy the fruits of their work in the past, their knowledge, passion, and finances to advance the causes close to their heart. In this stage, one should always remember the dreamer stage, dedicate life to a purpose, and help others.

In the present context, this book will cover childhood which is a part of the dreamer and explorer stages in respect of the childhood mind and education. It is also contemplated to identify the challenges encountered and the possible ways to reframe them to create opportunities and a strong foundation for the subsequent phases of life. In this phase of life, the challenges are faced by the child and the parents, teachers, educators, and the mental and mindset reconstructionist. It is the overall responsibility of all of them to help and guide the child to adopt the right path in their career and life for success, fulfilment, and happiness.

CHAPTER 3

Life itself is a challenge

"Where there is no struggle, there is no strength."
~ Oprah Winfrey

"Our greatest weakness lies in giving up.
The most certain way to succeed is always
to try just one more time."
~Thomas Edison

Life is itself a Challenge. The challenges come in many faces and magnitudes, in every walk of life at various stages from birth to the end of the journey of life. Challenges are equally there from childhood to adulthood. Challenges exist in every sphere of life in the fight for health and happiness, education, work, and relationships. A great deal of mental effort is required to accept these challenges and do away with life's strenuous journey. Coming out successfully despite the multifaceted challenges is the test of a person's mental strength and ability to face varied situations.

Childhood is a most sensitive and delicate stage of life. It is full of awesome challenges which lie ahead. Settling down with positive outcomes and achievements of the desired results and goals can happen with the support and guidance of the parents and teachers and the child's undeterred willpower to win over.

In the past, childhood was more akin to nature and simplicity of understanding the world and relation with their parents. Today, however, children and young ones seem to pose challenges to their parents' viewpoints, arguments, authority, and even beliefs. There is no fault in them. This is rather a demand for change that is taking place in the evolutionary behaviours of human nature to cope with the ever-changing environment of the world and its inhabitants.

Today, being at the mentor age, I see my past, recollect every moment, and analyse it. I can recollect everything that I have passed through and try to learn. I have learned at every moment, every situation, and every action, be it good or bad, success or failure, productive or otherwise; I have always tried to learn from my childhood till today.

It was my habit to learn from my mistakes and others' failures. I also had the habit of identifying my fault and weaknesses besides trying to see the challenges in doing anything good for me, my family, my society, and the institutions I am associated with and obliged to. I am never afraid of fighting to overcome challenges. Fighting for a cause gives me strength, and the achievements, be they exceedingly small, make me happy. My happiness doubled when it came to the challenges to be overcome for my society and my colleagues.

I remember the people I served in every walk of life, the students I taught, mentored, and cared for, and I tried to make them human and see them established in life. I realize I still have a long way to go, and they need me.

Challenges I faced at my schools: My Childhood mental journey

The memories of my childhood in my native village, where I lived with my grandparents, uncles, and cousins, are always with me. My grandfather, who never had the opportunity to attend school, taught me valuable lessons through his life experiences. He was deeply connected to the land, air, and water and worked hard to provide for our family while maintaining his dignity and that of our community. He allowed me the freedom to make mistakes and learn from them. I promised myself that I would keep these lessons close to my heart and, if given the opportunity, pass them on to future generations and my students.

My childhood education in places like a remote village Keotkuchi, a small hilly hamlet Along, and a small township Nowgong also left a lasting impression on me, and I strive to incorporate these experiences into my life.

Today I go back to my childhood, those uncared-for days and schooling. I try to enumerate some of my thoughts about the challenges of my mind and education, trying to seek how the mind map could be drawn for the upcoming generations in the present day circumstances.

CHAPTER 4

Brain and Mindset development in a child

"Twenty years from now, you will be more disappointed by the things that you didn't do than by the ones you
did do. So..... sail away from the safe harbor. Explore. Dream. Discover"

~Mark Twain

Biologically a child's brain develops more from birth to five years of age than in any other period of life. About 90 percent of the brain's growth occurs during this age period. This early act of brain development causes a permanent and continued impact on a child's ability to learn during life. The quality of a child's experiences in the first few years of life, positive or negative, greatly influences the brain and its development and activities.

The brain is the main centre for controlling every function of the body of humans. The new born baby develops all the brain cells, called neurons which remain for their entire life. These brain cells' networking (synapses) takes place during early childhood. This makes the brain function for all body activities and does everything, like physical movement, communication, and thinking processes. Different areas or parts of the brain regulate physical and mental functions. The connections between the brain cells need to be normal and healthy. This is required to perform all the complex processes by the individual during their life to enable them to move, speak and think normally and efficiently. Many important higher-level abilities like motivation, self-regulation, problem-solving, and communication are also formed in these early childhoods.

Contacts and relationships with their parents and others, including teachers and other community members, influence the development of the child's brain and their response to normal health. Providing the required love, care, and the most suitable environment is crucial to a child's brain development and function.

Developmental domains of childhood

According to the education expert, the five developmental domains of childhood are:

1. Physical: the development process of the child's biological and physical features and functions.

2. Social: the way a child interacts and behaves with others, understanding their duties and responsibilities as members of their own families and communities, as well as the ability to relate to their own and others' work.

3. Emotional: the process adopted by a child to create emotional bonding with others and develops self-confidence. Emotional connections can develop when the child can relate to other people and share feelings with friends.

4. Language: how the child communicates their feelings and emotions to others and how they express them to themselves. At 3 months, children use different crying modes for different needs. At 6 months, they recognize and imitate the basic sounds of

spoken language. In the first 3 years, children should be exposed to communication to pick up spoken words, vocabulary acquisition, and language.

5. Cognitive skills: This is the process in which a child learns to organize information and structure it. Some initial cognitive skills are problem-solving, creativity, imagination, memory, and recitation. They also start to retain a sense of the world. The children, however, differs in exhibiting their thought process and patterns as they move through different stages of cognitive development during the sensorimotor period, the pre-operational period, and the operational period.

To acquire the developmental domains, a child must be given the essential needs for learning and education.

Childhood Mindset and experience

It is said that the child experiencing a healthy and positive environment and interactions in their early years become physically and mentally healthier and more resourceful. They achieve success during their school life and education as well. It is also observed that some children perform well despite their deprivation. However, the lack of proper learning experience and atmosphere in a family due to unwanted situations adversely affects the mind and mindset of the child. Lack of appropriate and positive psychological and moral boosting also causes the child to suffer from negativity and lack initiative. This, on many occasions, leads the child to become a nonperformer.

The mentally healthy child having a positive interaction with love and care during early childhood attain their developmental and emotional traits quickly. They also learn the required individual and social skills. These help them achieve the power to adjust in any difficult situation and resolve many of their problems through their own efforts. The child is then almost ready to express their mindset. They gradually start to form beliefs about themselves as early as three years of age. This development of the character of believing in self about their intelligence, talents, abilities, and confidence creates their mindsets. Together all these characteristics impact the child's motivation, self-regulation, and independent thinking, which results in their achievements and success.

CHAPTER 5

Childhood Education and the Role of Teachers

"Education is not the learning of facts, but the training of the mind to think!"

~ Albert Einstein

Childhood education is receiving or giving systematic instruction, especially at an educational institution. In other words, education is the act of teaching and imparting knowledge to others and receiving knowledge from someone else. Education also refers to the knowledge received through schooling or instruction from any teaching institution. It is achieving knowledge, values, skills, beliefs, and moral habits. With the changing need of the world and the sustainability of life and life process, a human being needs to get a high level of awareness about the importance of knowing more than ever before.

During the period from birth to eight years of age, remarkable brain development takes place in children. During this stage, a crucial opening and opportunity are needed for education. United Nations Educational and Cultural Organization (UNESCO) believes early childhood care and education (ECCE) is truly inclusive. It is much more than just preparation for primary school. It can be the foundation for emotional well-being and learning in different phases throughout life.

During early childhood, a child cannot foresee the meaning of the instructions or guidance given by the parents or teachers in theoretical or application terms. But they can follow the same when they see immediate results and benefit from it. However, it is the moral responsibility and duty of the teacher or educator to explore the individual interest and capability of the child to impart education and guidance to the child. The teacher should also see and ensure that each child obtains the information essential to his personal and individual development.

Role of schools and Teachers

The teacher in a school is the first formal educator in the learning process and the knowledge giver to the child. The basic aim of the teachers dealing with childhood in any school is to handle the psychology of the children expressing their behavior regarding different traits of a human being. The teachers also need to understand every child's interest, capability, and desire to perform any activity or work by the child.

The genetics of every child is different; therefore, the ultimate expression of their characters is also different. These are further complicated due to the genetic and environmental interaction in ultimate and observable characteristics and efficiency performed by the child. Therefore, the role of the teachers and parents becomes highly critical in understanding the children.

It is not that at this stage only the textbook lessons will be able to deliver education, as a matter of fact, knowledge and wisdom. It is the innovative methodology and techniques of dealing with the child psychology matters on the part of the teacher while imparting education for developing the child into a complete human being.

The aim of the process and delivery of education by the schools is to empower the child with knowledge and wisdom. Knowledge is information that someone is aware of to build confidence in understanding a subject. This provides the potential ability to use it for a specific purpose in any field and for human welfare. In the process, the child gradually develops wisdom as he grows. Gradually the child acquires the ability to make correct judgments and decisions. It is an intangible quality gained through the guidance of teachers, parents, and mentors and, above all, by experiences in different phases of life.

Fifteen (15) qualities of the teachers of early education

The fifteen most vital qualities of the teachers of early education which can make a difference in the lives of children are:

1. Passion for teaching and dissemination of knowledge,

2. Love for the children and their well-being,

3. Patience and perseverance,

4. Possess the quality of caring and

compassion,

5. Flexibility with well-organized and well-framed plans,

6. Empathy for the children for their emotions,

7. Should possess the creativity and thinking mind,

8. The capability of providing the required comfort with arts and crafts,

9. Art of storytelling, conducting exercises,

10. The capacity to create the storyline for each lesson,

11. Ways of a structural and systematic approach for educational games and instructions,

12. The capability of organizational skills to make life easy for all,

13. Communication efficiency, along with listening skills and moods,

14. Understanding the inner meaning of the expressions of the children,

15. Dedication to help the child grow mentally and intellectually to become successful.

The teachers should be aware that they will face challenges and opportunities in imparting education for early childhood. Early childhood education teachers must be resilient to adversities and challenges to produce a human being in the child. This can happen by keeping their passion for guiding the children throughout their mental journey of education. It is an exceedingly difficult, cumbersome, and strenuous task to accomplish. By any means, it requires the devotion and dedication of a special person. In this endeavour, the support and cooperation of individual communities and society are of utmost importance. One should also be clear that this is an investment made for the future.

CHAPTER 6

Genetics, family, and the Child

"Genes are like the story, and DNA is the language that the story is written in."

Sam Kean

Development of the characters or expression of traits of biological, physiological, behavioural, or intelligence in human beings takes place through the inheritance of genes. Genes are the unit of heredity. They are responsible for transferring characters from the parents to the offspring.

Genetic conditions are often hereditary because they can be passed from parents to their children. However, the characters expressed may differ in the sons and daughters due to varying expressions of the genes and their interaction. Like most aspects of human behaviour and cognition, intelligence is a complex trait influenced by genetic and environmental factors. Similarly, personality traits like extraversion, neuroticism, agreeableness, conscientiousness, and openness are also genetic.

Genes are the basic physical and functional units of heredity and are responsible for developing the characters in humans, animals, and plants. Genes are in the chromosomes of the human body cells and consist of Deoxyribonucleic acid (DNA); they vary in size from a few hundred DNA bases to more than two million bases in one gene. Every person has two copies of each gene, one inherited from each parent.

A child inherits a set of 23 chromosomes from the mother and another 23 from the father. One of those pairs is the chromosomes that determine the biological sex of a child; girls have an XX pair, and boys have an XY pair.

Many genes are involved in developing and expressing a character or trait. There is not a specific gene that determines overall cognitive function; rather, it is developed due to the action of many genes.

Intelligence is a complex trait, meaning multiple alleles and several genes work together to determine a person's IQ score. Like most aspects of human behaviour and cognition, intelligence expression is influenced by genetic and environmental factors.

Intelligence is a challenging subject because it can be defined and measured differently. Current neuroscience research suggests that most new born have the potential to achieve in many cognitive areas. There will be some genetic predispositions, but the child's brain is extraordinarily malleable and "teachable." Therefore, the intelligence and merit of a person depend on both hereditary and environmental interactions to which the child is exposed for education, training, and practice for utilization of the brain to the maximum possible extent.

For example, I am putting some real-life stories to exemplify this and childhood activities, actions, and experiences to corroborate the views and explanations about childhood challenges and the approaches to overcoming them.

Mother (Maternal genetics)

Mother is the soul of a family.

My mother read up to class IV only. She could write and read-only Assamese, my mother tongue. She was from a big merchant family, i.e., the early 1940s hailing from Tarabari in Assam, India. The place was on the southern bank of the mighty Brahmaputra in lower Assam. My maternal grandfather had four brothers, all of whom were merchants professionally. They used to travel west by the Brahmaputra in big boats loaded with merchandise items. They used to move for a couple of months from Tarabari towards east Bengal, now parts of Bangladesh and west Bengal, through the river route. They do business, sell their items, and buy others in river ports. They return by the river route again with their money earned all-cash in coins in several jute bags. This was their routine affairs and business for livelihood and family maintenance and welfare. All four brothers had a joint family of about twenty-six members and lived in a big palatial house built in the form of the famous Assam-type architecture with British touch in the design. The houses with thick walls were built on about two acres of land. I still remember the wooden structures of the house and furniture constructed with highly artistic native 'Jalikota' designs.

My mother had four sisters, none of whom had any formal school education. In its true sense, there was no custom or compulsion for women's formal education at that time. Still, they were given the facilities of up to primary level education through some lower primary school or private tutors, which my grandfather very well afforded. She wrote many letters in Assamese to me when I was in different places in the country and abroad for my education.

My mother was an amazingly simple, innocent, and kind-hearted woman. All her sisters and cousins were similar in their character, and they were dear to the entire family and the village. On the other hand, her brothers all got their education in formal schools, and most of them had higher education and degrees in Calcutta (now Kolkata); they occupied many big and responsible positions later in the British era and independent India.

I heard many stories about my maternal grandfather's family from my mother and enjoyed with thrills about the life of that time people and astound to know these. She was married to my father in 1947 after his release from the British Indian army after World War II was over.

Father (Paternal genetics)

Father is the life of a family.

My father hailed from a village known as Keotkuchi at that time, Kamrup district of Assam, which was about 40 km away from Tarabari, and he was one of the three sons of my paternal grandfather. My grandfather was a cultivator. He, however, hailed from another big family of artists who were performers in various sociocultural and religious functions and was in great demand now and then in the locality and the district.

My father was an ex-army man serving the British Indian army from 1942 to 1947 during the Second World War. He was a Matriculate from one of the oldest schools established during the British time in Barpeta town of Assam. He was exceptionally good in English and had a command of the language. He was recruited into British Indian Army in 1942 until the War was over and released from the army.

After his return to his native place of Keotkuchi, Barpeta, he married my mother in 1947 and started living in his native village of Keotkuchi. He received three war medals which he treasured as a testimonial to his service to the country. He has donated almost all the possessions of his army service to the people of the village and nearby areas.

I am the eldest son of our family. After my birth, our family moved to Shillong, the capital town of that time, undivided Assam, located in the Khasi and Jayanti hill districts. Our house was made of pine wood structure on a small hilltop surrounded by a wooden fence with a gate.

I was a small child, and we spent a few years there. I was most of the time taken care of by one Khasi lady. Everybody called her Kong, meaning sister. Shillong is a hill station, and during the British time, it was the region's summer capital. The fascinating scenic beauty, hills, pine trees, meadows, and wild grasses attracted my young heart to these creations of nature. It also instilled a permanent and deep feeling for nature in my mind, and I later indulged in it.

I was fascinated to hear the wartime (World War II) stories from my father when I was a young kid and even after I grew up. These stories of his at the time of turbulent situations all over the world and his narratives were so thought-provoking that even today, these have been a guiding factor in my life to face challenges of any kind, come what may. His journey from a remote village of Assam to Dhaka and then via Calcutta to Singapore with his battalion on a ship crossing the Bay of Bengal was hilarious. The breathtaking incidence of air attack and bombing in the fleet of ships was narrated by him on several occasions and about the causalities. Stories of their fighting in the alien land of Rangoon, Burma, and Singapore in the deadly war were gruesome. They have faced many causalities, but my father survived many onslaughts and eventualities. He talked about the stories of their captured soldiers of armies from other countries, particularly the Japanese soldiers.

My father was a very strict and disciplined person as I knew him. But he was very brave and kind-hearted; because of this, he was liked by all during his later phases. While listening to the stories about the war prisoners when my father and his battalion were camping in Singapore, I wanted to know about the psychology and feelings of the war prisoners they captured. It was heartening to know that the Japanese prisoners said to my father in broken English that "Indian masters good, others not good," quite naturally due to his behavioural differences and attitude even towards the enemy country and their soldiers.

After his return from the army in 1947, my father later had training as Surveyor and joined the civil service for the state of Assam. He has been deputed to NEFA (Northeast Frontier Agency) with his HQs at Aalong, now in Arunachal Pradesh of India. He joined there and shifted our family to Aalong.

There was no road connectivity from Assam to NEFA then as hills covered it with different ranges of altitude from subtropical to temperate Himalayan climate. My mother, grandmother, and two brothers went to Aalong by air in Dakota aircraft used by the army from Rowriah military air base located at Jorhat.

Later on, in his civil service engagement as a Surveyor and Overseer, he earned a good name and reputation because of his sincerity and brilliant service delivery to the Government of India at NEFA and Assam.

CHAPTER 7

My mind, love of nature, and the start of formal schooling

"Nature is a tool to get children to experience not just the wider world, but themselves."

~ Stephen Moss

In this book, I will be dealing with the relevant areas of childhood school education till the pre-dreamer stage of life while trying to emphasize the various facets and considerations required for delivering better education to children.

In the process, I am trying to narrate some of my childhood mental journeys and psychological ups and downs leading to changes in behavioural patterns while facing real-life situations.

Then I will try to explain these with the scientific and social understanding of the issues. In the process, I am also trying to explore and understand the challenges immersed and encountered and the approaches that need to be designed and followed to overcome, mitigate, or redraft the challenges to empower children and childhood education.

An effort has also been made to assist in the development of resilience of childhood education against the changes in the societal mindset and environmental ecology of the coming generations.

In this chapter, I am recollecting to narrate my childhood education journey till I went to primary school after making a lot of struggles to assimilate into the formal education system. But before that, I would like to narrate something about my family background, which substantially impacted my mental health and journey from childhood to step at the door of the subsequent educational journey.

My story of love for nature and early education

I have always felt a deep connection to nature. As a child, I spent much of my time outdoors, particularly in Aalong, NEFA. In 1954, when I was just five years old, I would walk to school with my friends from the Abor or Adi community. We took a small trail through meadows and grasslands, surrounded by lush green and blue hills. My friends would often walk ahead, but I would slow down, not wanting to leave the beauty of nature behind. I didn't enjoy being confined to my school for the whole day. I wanted to be free to play and explore the natural world. The smell of the soil after a rain, the feeling of raindrops on my skin, and the distant view of blue hills and clouds in the sky were all things that brought me joy.

When my quest to see and live on nature's lap is over for the day, I proceed to my school all alone. When I reach the school, I am invariably punished for coming extremely late. But I did not mind because I felt happy that I enjoyed and lived with my mother nature.

My teacher would ask me every day why I was late.

I did not want to lie and say, "I was with my mother."

My teacher would say, "How can it be, Netan? Your friend said that both of you came together, but suddenly you disappeared on the way".

"Yes, Sir, he is right, but then I saw some beautiful

birds in the sky resting in a tree."

"So what, Dharma, did not you know that you would be late for school."

"Yes sir, I am sorry," I said in a trimmed voice. How can I tell him I cannot leave the scene in which I felt so happy?

This happens now and then.

I used to join my classmates on their way back from school as if I did not miss anything and headed towards our home.

I often spent my days near the riverside or small streams flowing from the hills to the valley where my school was located. I would observe the scenery, including the small huts and the people living there, and ponder the connection between them and nature. I didn't always understand my thoughts and feelings, but I felt content and happy in the vastness of the environment in front of me. I would sometimes discuss these experiences with my mother and try to understand more about what I was seeing.

Sometimes, I tell my mother to come with me to show her what I see and ask many things that come to mind. I wished to ask and know from her many things about the sky, about the trees, about the fresh and wet grasses and meadows, about the mist and fogs, about the wildflowers, about their mesmerizing smell and colors, about the clouds, about the small dancing streams, about the beautiful creatures, butterflies, birds, about the man and women working around collecting something for their home and about their life and so on. I faced the challenge of understanding nature, and my mind was always busy trying to find out what it is and how it is about nature.

I have not been able to concentrate on my studies. It was, of course, obvious due to my frequent absence from classes. This was gradually becoming known to everybody in my school, both my schoolmates and teachers. But I did not know what to do; I could not live alone and detach myself from the open and vast nature where I had somehow found my life's great satisfaction and happiness. I was in the quest for happiness and satisfaction from nature and my wish to engorge with it. That was a big challenge for me trying to achieve happiness from mother nature.

My teacher asks me repeatedly, "Dharma, you must attend your classes regularly and with punctuality. You must learn the lessons. You must pass the examination, then only you will be successful in life and earn a good name".

"Yes, sir. I shall obey you", I say, bowing my head.

I again fearfully add sometimes, "Sir, but I have some questions in my mind."

"OK, tell me," my teacher asks very fondly.

"Sir, nature is so dear to me; I love nature, I want to know and understand it, I want to live with it, sir; can you help me?"

"Yes, Dharma, I can help you, but you should not miss the regular school days."

"As because you need to study before you try to understand what you see there," my teacher added, "One day, we will go to see all the things there, and I will try to explain, not only to you but to all my pupils."

"Are you happy now?" He further added.

'Yes, sir, but when we go, sir, is it very soon? Which

way will we be going? We will go toward Siang Riverside, sir; I know all the places on that side", I uttered in one breath, expressing my overwhelming state of mind.

I always tried to derive happiness as much as possible from mother nature.

We were about fifteen students accompanied by our teacher on the weekend and went for a visit rather than our expedition.

We all assembled on the school premises early in the morning with a light bag containing food items.

While giving me the bag at home, my mother said, "Take your food in time, don't forget as you are in the habit of doing so while in the forest or somewhere."

"Take care, my dear, and come back home early," My mother said.

My father has already talked to my teacher yesterday and took stock of the position of all arrangements, routes, and about safety all along.

He said, "Stay all of you together and don't leave

the company of your teacher and follow his instructions."

"Yes, Maa-Deuta," I said a bit unmindfully and said "Bye" to them as I was in a different world, thinking about our trip all the time.

We all started at the school. That was a very misty and foggy November morning.

Our teacher guided us. Our family assistant, Kaw, a local man of the Adi community, had also accompanied us. He was an honest and trusted person lived with our family and an accompaniment of my father for a long time during our stay in NEFA, now known as Arunachal Pradesh in India.

We tracked down about 5 km on that day. I was thrilled to be with nature. I was doubly excited when our teacher explained about the trees, grasses, meadows, wildflowers, orchids, leaves, butterflies, animals, insects, fruits, rivers, streams, cold water of the rivulet, and whatnot. He explained the life of the trees and plants, their association with us, and why we should love them. I was surprised when we were told that we cannot live without the trees. At that time, I could not understand how. But when I grew up, I realized the fact.

During my childhood days, I was, in fact, inseparable from nature. On that day, I had many questions and tried to seek answers from my teacher. He explained, and I tried to realize, although it was difficult for me to grasp many of his explanations at that time.

At one point in time, I also asked many things to my friends and to Kaw, who had all along accompanied and helped other students and me in climbing stiff lands and hilly slopes. Kaw was a local tribal person, and his company has enhanced my joy of getting answers to my inquisitiveness.

After noon while traveling towards the deeper wood, I suddenly realized that I was separated from my other friends and only Kaw was with me. He was the only man with me and asked if we should join the group somewhere. But then I was so excited about his company and real-world nature I said to him, "Kaw uncle, we will go towards the riverside."

He said, "Riverside is a little far from this place."

"No matter," I said. "I want to go and see the river

and fishes."

We walked down towards the riverside. I saw the river full of stones of different sizes and shapes. How fascinating it was to see the water coming down striking the stones, we walked through, and I enjoyed the thrilling and strong touches of the water drops.

Kaw held my hand and helped me to cross one stone after another. I feel I am the happiest person in the world that day.

I told Kaw, "Uncle, let us go downstream. Let me see the river full of water and waves.

Kaw said, "We will then be late and unable to join the group."

I said, "It does not matter; we will join them upon our return to the school."

"But then your teacher will be annoyed, and it will not be a good thing to do," Kaw's uncle said.

But I insisted on him saying, "My sir knows me, it's ok. We will join them soon."

"Oh' fantastic, see the river down below the slope.

Full of water and flowing so calm." I shouted to him.

He said, "Yes, this river flows toward your school's valley."

"Let's go through this side to my school; I will surprise my teachers and classmates," I said.

"But then, in that case, we must cross the river. It is very deep this side", Kaw uncle said.

We went to the bank of the river and removed my shoes. I felt the sands pricking my feet below. It was a feeling I never forgot in my life.

The water was crystal clear. I saw everything in the waterbed, Colorful small stones and sands, some plants, mostly algae, and most fascinating small fishes swimming and jumping. I wanted to swim with them.

"Don't go beyond, Dharma," Kaw uncle shouted and held my hand.

"Let us go back, and join them. They must be worried thinking about us".

"Ok, but we have come far away from them," Kaw uncle said.

"Let's do one thing. If we cross the river from here, we will be able to reach your school before them", Kaw explained, pointing out the route with his finger.

I agreed and said, "How would we cross the river"?

"We have to swim and cross the river," he said.

I looked at the tiny fishes and was excited to see them swimming joyfully and enjoying their life.

"But how? I don't know how to swim; I am afraid I can't do that" I was really afraid of the situation at that moment. I felt that I had done a wrong thing by leaving our group.

But Kaw's uncle seems to be a fearless and worry less person. He said, "I will swim; you just sit on my back and hold my neck hard."

I was afraid of doing that, but there was no way out. I did that and grasped his neck, sat, and lay down on his back. He then started swimming. Gradually we were in the mid of the river, waves and water all the time sprinkled on my head, eyes, body, and everywhere. But I hold him so tight that I don't go out of his back. I closed my eyes most of the time, fearing something wrong.

I thought I would not be alive on that day.

Kaw uncle was a strong man possessing a strong and stout body which gave me confidence.

We crossed the river, and I lay down on the bank of the river. I was astonished about the act that I did not know how we did cross the river.

When we reached my school, I saw my friends, and our teacher was reaching the school. I raised my hand before my teacher could locate me on the school premises.

However, my teacher warned me severely on that day for the incident and my behaviour and for not being in the group together all the time.

He said, "Dharma, you made a big mistake. You should have been there with the group all along. You must obey the instructions of your teachers and parents".

He added, "Thank God, nothing untoward happened, and you and we all are safe."

I felt guilty. I realized that I had broken the discipline. I could not utter a single word. But I think I have learned a lesson.

CHAPTER 8

My Struggling mind and Challenging school

"A child without education is like a bird without wings."

~Tibetan Proverb

"Challenges are what make life interesting. Overcoming them is what makes life meaningful."

~ Joshua J. Marine

I was not particularly interested in my academic study during my school education's pre-primary and primary stages.

Why I love nature, I realize now. And that was challenging to me whether I should be with nature all the time or study. Today, when I analysed and read the experts, I found that my emotional behaviour and approach toward life differed from that stage's present-day children. I think present-day parents are well equipped with the knowledge of bringing up their children. But then many more issues need to be taken care of.

I did not apparently have any problems then, but now I feel that I have some problems with emotional strengths. I analysed my childhood life now and tried to have some critical insight into the emotional status, strength, behaviors, and above all, challenges of my childhood.

As experts say, there are many challenges in childhood mind and education. These include insights into the child's emotional behaviour. Being experienced very little and new to the world at this stage, the children face many challenges. They are not mature enough to have a correct perspective of anything and live in their fantasy, imaginary, and magical world. These create a situation in their minds building a thought process that overpowers the process of understanding reality.

Most children are not mature enough and try to put things together that are unrelated and then form an illusionary correlation and try to follow. I made a mistake when I tried to ride a mule in the army camp without assistance after I read the story of 'Pakhiraj' and broke my leg after falling from his back at Aalong.

Being a young child is overwhelming, emotional, and sometimes amazing, but often frustrating when you need to adhere to parents' or teachers' rules. Yes, they probably know better, but we do not realize this when we are young. Sometimes we feel misunderstood because of our actions which are not desirable in the eyes of our parents. So, part of being a child means we do not have the whole picture, and the challenges mentioned are inherent to the experience of growing up.

These childhood challenges are very common irrespective of the child's race, nationality, religion, or culture and the nature of the upbringing by their parents. Many intrinsic and extrinsic factors obstruct the children in such a situation, and thereby they are unable to find out the right perspective of any situation and, therefore, unable to or inexperienced to resolve their issues and act differently. This used to occur due to inexperience in understanding the subject and perceiving exactly the situation they encounter and see, lack of knowledge and ability to handle the challenges and find out the alternatives, and lack of correct perception in mind.

I was very shy in my childhood. I felt trapped within the four walls of my school. I often avoid my way to school and leave all others in a different direction. To avoid school, I sometimes climbed some trees and spent my time as I was very fond of fresh fruits. All these activities were informed to my father by my schoolteacher.

One fine morning when I was to leave for school, my father said, "Dharma, from today onwards, you will go to school with your Headmaster."

This was a bolt from the blue to me. I know, our Headmaster sir always goes to our school on foot by the small road near our home.

"Yes, father. But I must go a little ahead of him with my friends to reach school earlier", I said in a low voice.

"No, I have requested him to take you along," my father said and ordered me to obey him.

I am very much afraid of my father as well as our headmaster. However, I had no other option.

I had been waiting for sir and followed him with a hesitant move.

"Dharma, come along, and I will give you some advice for your studies." He said in a dear voice that somewhat helped me to become a little relaxed.

"Dharma, why don't you concentrate on your studies and try to learn whatever your teacher teaches. You have sufficient time to play and walk around once your main job is over".

"Yes, sir, I will do that." then I said in a low tone, "Sir, I want to see and know how things around us happen."

"What do you mean?" my sir asked.

"How do the plants grow in soil? Have they lived like us"? Why the flowers and fruits of all the plants are different? Why do flowers smell beautifully and differently?" I did not realize to whom I was talking. Somehow, I spoke spontaneously and then stopped after realizing my sense.

He then went on speaking many things to me about whatever I asked. But after hearing a couple of sentences from him, I lost my mind somewhere and did not hear anything later. I went to a different world of nature, following his footsteps towards our school.

I think this was another challenge in childhood: the children are trapped in school, feel suffocated, and want to live in a free environment.

They feel they are not free to choose their subject of liking.

This is one of the biggest challenges to the teachers and the school that the child's inner voice is not heard and taken care of. It is also a challenge for the child to handle the situation so early in life.

I was affected by these feelings, although I could not express and communicate myself to my teachers.

I was physically healthy in my childhood as I was very fondly taken care of by my parents, providing me with good food and nursing. But somehow, perhaps, I do not know; my emotional health was probably overlooked because I was not fully acquainted with the basic need for mental strength to overcome every difficult or critical situation, making me weak in capturing the knowledge and wisdom for every situation.

The challenges I faced during my childhood were:

1. I was not particularly eager to study, rather wanted to be free to live with nature, vegetation, animals, flowers, blue sky, roaming clouds, rain, river, wild grasses, and whatnot.

2. I felt dull, depressed, and unhappy when restrained in the four walls of schools or homes.

3. I was not sharp enough to understand what my teachers said and explained.

4. I loved living alone in solitude or with those who liked me the most.

I now realize that we need to reframe these challenges to draw attention to the teaching and parenting strategies as a resource towards fulfilment and happiness.

CHAPTER 9

My mental journey - Fighting school education in varied atmospheres

"The purpose of learning is growth, and our minds, unlike our bodies, can continue growing as we continue to live."

~Mortimer Adler

Life is a Challenge. Challenges are equally there from childhood to adulthood. To accept these challenges and do away with life's strenuous journey, a great deal of mental or physical effort is required. Coming out successfully despite the multifaceted challenges is the test of a person's mental strength and ability to face the situation.

From Aalong (NEFA) to Keotkuchi (Assam) in search of a better field of my study

I spent about a year in my native village of Keotkuchi in the village primary school. My father thought that I might cope well in my native place and school and would be able to concentrate on my studies. When I was to leave my family at Aalong on that Dakota flight from Aalong to Rowriah airstrip near Jorhat town, my mother was very sad to leave me.

She grabbed me in her breast and said, "I love you, dear; I will join you very soon. Listen to your uncle there and go to your school regularly and study well".

I did not know what was happening and why I was to leave Aalong, NEFA, and go to my village in Assam. However, my parents were still there at Aalong. I was weeping, not exactly to leave my parents; my heart was breaking as I left behind my dearest nature, hills, streams, rivers, trees, grasslands, meadows, animals, birds, and everything.

I just took shelter in my mother's breast and was weeping.

I told her, "Please don't let me go; I will stay here with you and obey my dad and go to school."

I continued, "I will not see anything else; I will listen to my teachers and study."

I added, "Maa, I cannot leave my world here, and my heart goes for it here. Please do not send me anywhere".

My mother somehow consoled me, saying, "You will come back again, and we will live together. Be a good boy".

I realize today that my father was thinking about my betterment and becoming a good boy, concentrating on my study, and I think he was looking for a bright future for me. I thought that was his desire to think for me at that time. Because there was a time he struggled for his education and well-being before joining the army just after his Matriculation.

Two of my maternal uncles, after completing their school education, studied for degree programs during the latter part of the nineteen forties.

My eldest uncle completed his Law degree and my

younger uncle completed graduation in Anthropology from Calcutta and later became a District Judge in Assam, and a Professor after India's independence.

My father had the challenging task of training as a surveyor after his release from British Indian Army in 1947. He was then appointed as a surveyor and became an active member of the team of officers and workers assigned to construct the new airstrip at Aalong to improve the connectivity of NEFA with the rest of the country, as there were no other ways for communication at that time.

My challenge was, however, something else that is to take my life course living with nature and enjoying the beauties of nature as a part of it.

Today, when I retrospect, I understand the psychology behind this feeling of mine and the challenges I faced but could not cope with and resolve.

Now after spending my entire life as an academician and a motivator to my students and handling their mental agonies all the time, I realize and understand the situation when my father had to make all the decisions.

It was, of course, obvious due to my frequent absence from classes. I could not overcome this and could not cope with the challenges of that period of my childhood.

My days at Keotkuchi

Keotkuchi was my father's birthplace, where he lived with his two brothers. They had one sister married to a schoolteacher in another village about 100 km away. My father was the eldest of all. His next younger brother was a cultivator and was with me all the time with my grandfather.

He also looked after all the land they had, and they worked together with my grandfather. The youngest brother studied till his Matriculation at Barpeta, the nearest town to the village.

When I came back from Aalong all alone, leaving behind my parents and two brothers, I joined them in my paternal native place at Keotkuchi. I was admitted to my village primary school.

Although I was very sad and disheartened about

leaving my world in Aalong, I tried to cope with the prevailing situation and environment at Keotkuchi.

My father had great respect from all the villagers and our relatives. I was becoming dearer to everybody, including all my school teachers, even if my father was away.

At that time, we did not have any furniture in the school. Our teacher used a small wooden table and a chair for him. We, the students, used to carry a small empty gunny bag from our homes and sit there on the floor in the school. We write in an earthen slate keeping it in our lap. We practiced handwriting in banana plant leaves using the rigid structure of the bird's feather and ink.

Initially, I attended my school regularly, and our teachers paid attention to me. But gradually, I lost my concentration and felt that everything was monotonous. I felt that I was missing something. I tried to find out what I wanted and what I was getting. I was again in search of something that I was missing.

Gradually my mind was again diverted from my studies. I always wanted to visit the agricultural field with my grandpa every time and wanted to do one or the other work to help him learn. My grandpa and uncles were not happy about that. In the meantime, my youngest uncle left for training in clothing and textile in Mahabaleswar after his education here. My grandpa also told me that my uncle was interested in beekeeping.

My grandpa had no formal education, and he was a cultivator all along. He did agricultural activities all year round and disposed of the produce in the weekly market alone.

The market was about 4-5 Km away from our home. I accompanied my grandpa to the market every week. One day before the market day, I tried to help him out of curiosity.

He had some assistants for the purpose. He carries the products in gunny bags on his shoulder. However, when the produce was heavy and more items were in bigger harvesting, he used to take those in our bullock cart to the market.

I had lost my concentration in my studies, and my

results in the examinations were not up to the mark. Gradually I lost interest, and this fell in my father's ear.

When my father came to know about the situation, one day he came from Aalong to our home at Keotkuchi and enquired about the matter. He sat with my grandpa and uncle in my presence. He also invited some of my schoolteachers to enquire about the matter and decide what to do. Everybody in our village knew and liked my father for his helpful and benevolent nature, and everybody tried to help him. They took the matter very seriously and discussed it at length.

That was an excessively big day for me. I am usually very much afraid of my father and the teachers at my school. I was unable to give an appropriate answer to any of their questions.

My father asked, "My son, why don't you concentrate on your study? What is your problem?"

I said after a couple of minutes' silence, "Father, I do not know," but something is pulling me from behind, and I have become unable to stabilize my mind."

I paused; I did not know what the right answer would be. I knew that I could not express myself to them and that I could not explain my state of mind.

My teacher then asked me caringly and expressed great concern, "My dear Dharma, we are with you to remove if you are facing any problem and are finding yourself in a dilemma in your thinking."

Another teacher added, "We are with you to resolve any difficulty or inconvenience you are facing to free you from the hurdles, if any, in your approach to becoming a good student."

I was listening to them very carefully and thought to speak my mind.

I knew from my inner self that I did not have confidence in myself for anything and was afraid to express myself wrongly. I think because of that, I was unable to speak out. However, I try to analyse any matter or questions meticulously and, do that in my mind and inner self. But I was afraid of answering. Every time it comes to my mind that I should not be wrong, and that is the factor that makes me hesitant to answer or explain. As a result, I have become an introvert most of the time. People thereby misunderstand me and develop the impression that I have no knowledge and that my academic standing and IQ are extremely low.

My father always wanted me to be a very sincere and disciplined boy. He wanted me to help in my journey and told my teachers that he dreamed of making me a well-educated person and acquiring a responsible position in society.

But I was not able to deliver during those days because I have not been able to concentrate on my studies and wanted to do anything that came to me in front.

I knew that I was not focused on anything. But on the other hand, my father had a very sharp vision and target of doing things. I think he has acquired this quality from his military training during his days in the army.

I spoke to my father and the teachers very politely but a bit confidently, "I will improve my performance and study hard," but at the same time said to my inner self that I must do that, and I will do that by any means.

My father and the teachers then narrated some of

their experiences of their childhood and younger days and tried to convince me about what actions and mindset I should develop to succeed in life.

I was overwhelmed with their love and caring bits of advice, and listening to them; I could not but assure them and promise that I would do whatever was desired and expected by them.

I could not check the tears rolling down from my eyes. I did not try to wipe them out as I was feeling something very fulfilling and satisfying looking into my father's eyes.

The next day, my father left for Aalong again, getting my mind and assurances.

CHAPTER 10

My mental journey – Life's lessons learned from grandpa

"Every child needs a parent, grandparent, or friend who will say, let's go; it's time for an adventure."

~Penny Whitehouse

One day, I hesitatingly went to my grandfather and said, "Grandpa, I want to see your field. Would you show me what you do there?"

I noticed that my grandfather frequently leaves the house early in the morning with a plough in his shoulder and other implements and comes at noon or even later. He was very fond of me, but I missed him so much.

He kissed me and said, gently rubbering my head

and making my hair orderly, "I go to our field, my dear."

"What do you do there? I immediately asked him and promptly said without waiting for his answer, "I want to go tomorrow with you and see myself."

"Ok, but tomorrow you have to go to your school; you go with me on Sunday," he said.

"Yes, I agree, but you must take me to the field, Promise?" I demanded, and he assured me.

"Yes, I promise," My grandfather assured.

"But then you must get up from bed early and before sunrise, " he added.

However, I was surprised and excited and pondered why it was so early. But I was expecting something very thrilling.

That was the Sunday I had never seen a day earlier like that.

I slept with my grandpa the night before, and he woke me up from my bed. I opened my eyes hesitatingly with great difficulty.

It was literary dark inside our room. Still, then I opened my eyes and tried to feel the atmosphere.

My grandfather was already outside when I got out of bed. He called me and said, "Dharma, come on and see the outside."

I was out of the room and saw it was still not visible outside.

My grandpa said, "Wait for some time; the dawn is yet to be broken."

After some time, I saw my grandfather with his plough and all other things on his shoulder and was ready to proceed with the pair of bullocks.

I was moving with him by the side of the bullocks through the bumpy and dusty village roads toward our open fields.

I then shouted to him, pointing my finger towards the eastern sky, "Grandpa, see that rising sun on the eastern horizon and beautiful colors of the sun rays,"

"See the birds flying past the sun," I continued, "See the long and descending shadows of the trees trying to play hide and seek with us."

"See that cattle herd going towards the field by ringing their bells in the necks" I was continuously trying to express my emotions by drawing his attention and seeking answers to all my questions about how it was happening.

"Grandpa, I will always come with you to see these beautiful moments of nature," I shouted.

"You must take me along wherever and whenever you go." I appealed to him in one breath.

My grandpa said, "Ok, my dear, I will surely do that, but then you have followed what I say."

"Sure, grandpa, I will do that, but I want to be with you all the time to see these moments and say 'Good morning, world' at every dawn.

After some time, I did not know when we reached the middle of the big open field when my grandpa said, "this is our field, our land where we cultivate grains and other crops.

"Grandpa, how will you do that? I also want to grow these", I said.

"Ok, I will teach you and show you how this is done slowly," Grandpa assured me.

Grandpa was busy ploughing the land for quite a long time.

I was roaming around him and chasing the white egret birds gathered around.

I tried to catch them, but they were unstoppable.

They also played with me while foraging and eating the grassroots and insects in the soil.

Almost every Sunday and holiday, I accompanied my grandpa to the field, observed, and tried to learn and understand about growing crops and vegetables.

My grandma used to bring some food for my grandpa, maybe after about three hours. I feel that he must be very hungry by that time. I am also hungry.

We sit in the shadow of a small but bushy tree.

I have seen my grandpa's face many times, trying to read his heart and imagine what is in his mind at that time, his expectation out of this hard work.

My grandma was a beautiful woman having a face that was so endearing.

With her fair complexion and bright face, I see her

glowing when the early morning sunrays strike her face with a bright reddish colour.

"What is there for today, grandma? I am very hungry," I said, asking her to give me something.

She gave the brass bowl rapped with a 'gamosha' to me and said, "This is for you" after opening it, and then the other bigger bowl to my grandpa.

Sometimes my grandpa, although he was not literate, talked about my studies so that his knowledge and wisdom were beyond comparison to the other those I met later.

He says, "Dharma, I know you are very innocent, and your heart is full of goodness which should be there with anybody to lead a peaceful life."

He then quickly added something before I could say that I had not clearly understood his words at that stage of my life.

He said, "You will not understand now what I am saying, but I am sure when you grow up and encounter all the eventualities of life, you will realize, and I always pray for good things to happen for you."

He added, "Your father is also a noble and helpful man. His help to all the villagers here and his dedication to his work and duties make us proud, and we all here live with that.

He paused for a moment and then added, "That brings happiness and helps us to lead a peaceful life."

I tried to see his eyes when he tried to cover his tears rolling down.

"That is why I wish to tell you that don't hurt that person. He has sacrificed his life for the family and our countrymen while fighting in the war." Grandpa continued, "He only desires that you should be a good person to be liked by everybody, and now you should study hard to become a good person."

"Grandpa, you once told me that you have never gone to school during your time, but then how do you know all these things," I asked.

"See, Dharma, the world is itself a school, and one's life is the teacher for him, even today, and it will always be so." He spoke.

I could not grasp the meaning of that at that

moment. But this statement is still there in my heart, and I am reminded of every moment of my life, even today.

Today, I engorge myself devoted to my work and service to the people, my students, and the oppressed. I love nature, the environment, people, and everything in the world to try to learn and acquire knowledge.

Grandpa said, "Always be humble to all the creatures of the earth and try to understand them and help them in their need. They also have the same right as the human being".

He further added, "This is the service to be rendered for which God has sent all of us to this world."

"Grandpa, I have not understood you and your words; I don't know why; I think I am very small now, but I have understood one thing I should listen to my father, my mother, and you all and follow your advice."

"You see, Dharma, life is not but challenges, and every day, every moment, you encounter one or the other. For instance, now you are to take the challenge of learning and educating yourself to equip you and to make you fit for taking any responsibility", he said with a very strong voice that seemed to echo from his heart.

Although I was only a small kid at that time, I don't know how my brain and heart took these words of my grandpa at that time.

I still remember those days with him quite vividly, and even today, I realize that those were the gospel of my life and gave me the directions and laid the foundation of my path of life.

Adaptation challenges: Movement from one school to another

"Education is the passport to the future, for tomorrow belongs to those who prepare for it today."

~ Malcolm X

Challenges of my adapting to the new setup at Nowgong moving from my native village Keotkuchi was initially a tough job for me.

I was pleased to be with my grandpa and grandma in Keotkuchi, a small village about 5km away from Barpeta town of Assam. Almost all the villagers were cultivators. There was one primary schools and one middle school in the village. But gradually, many of their wards moved to schools and colleges in other places and towns of Assam after their schooling.

My grandpa liked me a lot because I was very close to his heart. I always roam around him and try to help him in his day-to-day activities using my tiny pair of hands.

I gradually developed an interest in his works and was fascinated to see his care for growing crops and raising livestock and birds.

I keenly observed his works and tried to learn many things by seeing and doing.

My uncle, the younger brother of my father in our home, was another very skilled person in almost all areas of cultivation, growing and harvesting crops, and all other agricultural activities. Besides that, he was an expert fish catcher.

During the flood season, which was a natural phenomenon every year during monsoon. At night time, he takes out his small wooden boat and takes a lamp and a fishing spear for fishing.

I often used to go with him along with my grandpa. Although they were reluctant to take me with them at night on many occasions for that kind of activity, I forcefully took the opportunity to enjoy the night fishing adventure.

We usually go towards the flooded field by river water of at least 5-6 ft depth in many places

My grandpa normally takes the lamp with him and sits in the middle of the boat, and I sit at one end. My uncle used to hunt fish of big size with a spear when the fish came nearer to the light source.

A small fishing net was kept in the boat where the catch was kept securely. I have also seen some fish even escape and jump into the water. Sometimes I also used to release one or two such fishes into the water; I liked to see their strength and enjoy their jumping into the water for a new lease of life.

I still remember the bright flashes of the scales of the fish skins during the moonlit nights.

We return to our home invariably at midnight. The next day early morning, my grandpa and uncle used to sell their catches in high demand.

By the end of the second standard of my schooling in Keotkuchi, before the annual examination, one

day, my grandpa took me to another field that he had prepared for the cultivation of a new ground nut crop field that I did not see earlier. This land was situated by the side of the 'Chaulkhowa' river. There was a small hut in one corner of the field where my grandpa used to stay at night and guard the crops when they were almost ready for harvesting.

One day after making a round in the field and completing his work, particularly removing the weeds from the rows, we sat in the shade of a tree.

"Dharma, how do you like this land? It is very fertile, isn't it?" My grandpa said.

"What is the fertile"? I asked him; I heard something new.

He then went on to narrate about the soil and the factors responsible for increased crop production in terms of quality and quantity. However, I could not follow and understand at that time.

"The food we take should have all the basic ingredients required for our life process, health, and wellbeing. The plants acquire all the nutrients from the soil and produce food for us for our life and living", my grandpa said slowly.

"Nature, the environment, the atmosphere that we are in comprised of air, water and earth are God for us, and they give us life, feed us, care for us, and thereby we live," he tried to make me understand his words and feelings.

"That's why it becomes our duty to preserve and protect them, never neglect them and try to maintain their purity." He added, "Try to learn from them the pleasure of giving selflessly and ask for nothing in return, and be happy."

"I have not gone to school in my life; we have learned to love people from nature as you have seen, and till nature is with us in its full bloom, we are safe." He was narrating his stories looking to the sky and then his crops and the river as if he was still trying to understand many things that were still unknown to him.

I could realize that he had engorged deep into his feelings while trying to enrich his knowledge and wisdom for passing on to me.

Today, I think those were some of the most beautiful moments of my life; I cherished them throughout and even tried to percolate into the hearts of my students subsequently.

On many occasions, I accompanied my grandpa while returning from the field after work or returning home in the evening with the cattle and goats after their day-long grazing or carrying our headload of dry small tree branches or bushes for fuel for the fire.

He will carry a big load and give me a small bundle on my head, and I follow him to our home. I often do not see the road to a distance as my eyes are sometimes covered with dry leaves and when the load has to be kept in balance in my head, I follow his footsteps on the sandy roads to reach our home.

Today I remember this man whenever I am in a pensive mood in such a way that my heart goes to him as if, at that time, I was literary following his footsteps in life and livelihood. He tried to make me understand the philosophy of life.

The next day when I was preparing to return home from school, my class teacher came near to me and said, "Dharma, wait for a moment; we will go together."

I was a little worried; I don't know why. Yesterday he was with my grandpa for quite some time discussing something. Maybe they were discussing me, I presumed.

"Yes sir, I will wait for you and then go," I said politely and came out from our classroom slowly.

After some time, my class teacher told me to follow him towards our home. I saw all the school boys staring at us and talking about something among them, pointing towards me.

"Sir, have I done anything wrong," I asked my teacher as I could not resist my inquisitiveness anymore and looked at him fearfully.

These days I attend my school almost regularly and accompany my grandpa to the field after school or on holidays only. I also occasionally accompany him on the weekly market day afternoon.

"Not exactly, Dharma, I know. Your grandpa has called me to have some discussion." He spoke.

I then kept silent, thinking about what may be the matter. I have not made any mistakes.

I was accompanying my grandpa, trying to learn what he says and help him.

After about half an hour's walk, we reached our home. I saw my grandpa and grandma waiting in front of our house.

"Sir, namaskar, please come, " my grandpa said to my teacher, showed him the way towards our front yard, and requested him to sit in the wooden chair.

My grandma went in after wishing my teacher a Namaskar.

My grandpa took a small wooden stool and sat on that after my teacher took his chair.

"Dharma, you go in and take some food and then come after some time," my grandpa instructed me.

I went in, kept my books and slate on the table near my bed, and then went to wash my hands and feet. In the meantime, my grandma called me and gave me some food.

"Why my schoolteacher is coming, Grandma. I am very much afraid. I have done nothing wrong these days.

"Don't worry, Dharma, your grandpa will be discussing something about your study. He received a letter from your father a couple of days ago. I think he will discuss that." My grandma said.

I am relieved after hearing her.

I then went out and joined my grandpa outside in the front yard.

"Come on, Dharma," my teacher asked me to stand near him.

"Dear Dharma, I have good news for you." He said to me with a smile.

I was extremely excited and asked him, "Yes, sir."

My teacher asked my grandpa to reveal the news.

I asked, "What is that, Grandpa?"

"You will be joining your parents very soon and living together." He spoke.

My teacher added, "Your parents will be coming to Nowgong from Aalong after completing his assignment there very soon. Nowgong is an exceptionally good place, and there are some good schools. You will be admitted there along with your brothers."

"I am sure you will be there in a new place with a new school and new teachers and will like it," he continued.

He said, "Now is the time for your growth, and you should also try hard to develop your mental strength and study hard."

After seeing their face once, I said, "Yes, sir, what should I do about that?"

I know everybody says I am not good in studies; everybody ridicules me as and when I give wrong answers to any question".

"You must concentrate on your studies and develop your ability to work hard," Sir said in a strong advisory tone.

"Yes, sir, I will do that and listen to my father's and teachers' advice," I said.

But I was sad that I would miss my grandpa and my life with him. Although I will be in a new place with new environment and surroundings, my mind and heart will always be with him. I promise never to forget his teachings and words and follow him in times to come.

CHAPTER 12

Challenges of understanding new friends and relations

"My best friend is the one who brings out the best in me."

~Henry Ford

In 1956 we went to Nowgong, a town in middle Assam. My father, after leaving Aalong, joined in his service in the 'Khagarijan Aanchalik Panchayat' office as an Overseer to work for the construction and maintenance of roads and bridges under the state government.

My father also had a government quarter as his official residence. That was an L-shaped Assam type house with a thatch roof and ceilings made of bamboo. The walls were mud-plastered. Doors and windows were made of woods of local timbers of

Teak (Tectona Grandis) tree, while the posts were all made of 'sal' (Shorea robusta) trees. The house had a reasonably big compound where all sorts of vegetable gardening were done throughout the year.

After settling there, my father took us, my mother, me, and my two younger brothers, to Nowgong. I remember the day when our family was to leave my grandpa, grandma, and uncle at Keotkuchi.

"Remember Dharma, what I told you," my grandpa said with tears in his eyes. Then he further said, "I know you are an intelligent boy; you only need to focus on your target."

My grandma took me in her arms and said, "Don't be sad, you will come again, and we will live together."

Then she added, "listen to your father's advice and study hard." "You must be a big man and earn a good name for our family."

My mother touched the feet of my grandpa and grandma, and we departed with heavy hearts from our native village.

I still remember those days of spending with

grandpa, grandma, and uncle in that remote village amid all-natural bouts, my learnings, and the experience of understanding them with my very young brain and mind. I imprinted many things in my mind that provoked me to develop my mindset today to see the world, the people, and my attitude and approach toward life.

I was thinking to Nowgong about what was in my mind as the challenges of leaving my native village.

My father was a highly active person and was liked by all in the town for his military discipline, which he acquired in the British Indian army during the second world war.

Our family was close to an Anglo-Indian family living at Nowgong for a long time. My father was close to the family, and we had a close social relationship. We heard many stories of their life and tried to articulate some social human behaviours.

I also had a good friendship with their son, Boris, and we were in the same primary and high school classes. During his pre-primary classes, Boris read in the town Mission school. Later, when we became close to each other, Boris and I joined my school to study together.

During the day after school, we play together in the circuit house field and in their house. I always felt incredibly happy to be there due to the love and affection of his mother.

Boris was good in his studies but also unmindful about his classwork. We used to miss too many of our classes and could not pick up the lessons.

"How are your studies, Dharma?" Boris's father asked us one day before our class III final examination.

I was a little hesitant to answer for quite some time. I was thinking about what to say. My preparation was not up to the mark and my satisfaction. I will never tell a lie. I want to speak the truth, but then it will not be liked by him.

"It's ok, father," Boris replied. I am relieved.

"You see, my dear Boris and Dharma, your preparation and results of this particular entrance examination are very important to secure a place in the Government high school," Boris's father said in a very strong voice.

"We all want both of you to work hard," He added and said further, "Boris, you see, Dharma's father is a very intelligent and honest person; Dharma should not dishearten him."

Boris and I were together for our studies and played with other friends in the locality. Boris always used to take care of me in all matters. But still, then, I could not concentrate fully on my studies.

I have seen Boris's father and my father talk about me now and then, and they were concerned about me.

Looking at me one day again, Boris's father told me, "Why are you so hesitant to go to school? I have not seen your active involvement with your teachers. Is there any problem? Tell us, and we will try to resolve it".

I said, "I do not know. I cannot even make friends easily and share my feelings."

"Boris, can you help him," Boris's father told him.

"But at this moment, both of you concentrate on your studies to produce a good result." Boris's father continued and advised a lot many things.

A couple of days later, my father arranged for a home tutor for us. I was happy that Boris used to come regularly for that.

The first few days, it went on smoothly. Gradually I found it has become extremely hard for me to continue. Whenever our home tutor asked anything, Boris used to reply quickly, but I could not respond fast. I also find it difficult to memorize the complete lesson.

When Boris and I completed the year in class three, we appeared in the annual examination and waited for our results for a few days. When the results came, we found that our performance was mediocre.

My father said, "Now that your results are not good enough, you have to work hard to sit in the entrance examination for Class IV admission in the Government Higher Secondary school." The same was the case with Boris; his father also warned him.

Both of us appeared in the Government Higher Secondary school entrance test at Nowgong. But to our utter dismay, we could not figure in the selection list in both sections of class IV.

Boris's father met the School Headmaster and enquired about our performance.

"There is a decision at the school level that from this year onward, another section will be added with about 30 students, and admission will be given according to the merit-based test conducted", I heard Boris's father telling my father.

That was great news for both of us when my father told me we had seats in the newly opened Section C in class IV.

I was feeling relaxed and happy that we could take admission now.

I remember vividly today that it gave me a tremendous moral boost, and I felt I must try to improve my performance from now onward.

I also felt satisfaction and gained energy to start a new chapter in my life.

CHAPTER 13

Childhood Education Challenges

"Our challenge isn't so much to teach children about the natural world, but to find ways to sustain the instinctive connections they already carry."

~ Terry Krautwurst

Narrating some real-life stories and experiences of my childhood as described in the preceding chapters, I now try to explain the challenges during the stage of youth in general terms which are faced by any child, their parents, teachers, and educators.

It has also been tried to draw the mind map to redraft the challenges into opportunities for framing the future stages of life to lead a successful life and career.

It has also been tried to identify the specific challenges and gaps in childhood education.

Critical analysis of the challenges and to find out the possible strategies to adopt have also been made to overcome the challenges.

Well, thought and effective practices to achieve success, reach the goal of a successful career, and achieve happiness in life have been suggested.

Understanding Childhood Education

Education in childhood, as a matter of fact, the entire childhood activities, now faces a tremendous challenge.

The stakeholders in the education system find it a daunting task to understand the childhood education challenges and their possible resilience measures in the emerging social and economic divergence in today's world.

This threatens the social fabric of relationships and the stability of the welfare system and security.

Therefore, childhood educationists, teachers, parents, and society need to identify the gaps and develop and adapt suitable and well-thought policies and practices to reframe and address the challenges to create opportunities.

In childhood education, Nature first

This is invariably the feeling in early childhood to stay and live with nature. On many occasions, this act of childhood was misunderstood by their parents and teachers in the past. Of course, they are also not at fault. Because then, there was not much research or studies conducted to analyse child psychology, behaviour, mindset, and mental makeup.

Therefore, the childhood problems that occurred in earlier generations also occur today in one or the other forms with the children of contemporary generations.

This needs the attention of their parents, teachers, and educators.

Seven (7) issues and approaches for effective modulation of childhood and nature are

1. The most important aspect of childhood education is that they carry forward with nature and the environment from the beginning of their learning process.

2. Childhood education at this stage needs to be practiced in situ so that nature in real-life

situations could be brought nearer to their life.

3. Early childhood is always close to nature, and they behave as a part of that. This trait of the children needs to be inculcated and preserved in their lifelong learning so that human beings can coexist with nature in the future to save the planet from perishing.

4. They should also be taught at an incredibly early stage that there is no other alternative to mother nature.

5. It is high time that the challenge of this teaching-learning process must be carried forward with the desired course contents, study materials, and a proper and judicious education system.

6. The challenge in Early Childhood Education (ECE) must be combined with Education with Nature (EWN). The EWN will be a combined approach with flexibility and an easily understood scientific basis for explaining nature and the environment.

7. The EWN should be designed to conform to and suit different locality and their

individualized educational essentialities.

Educating with Nature

We need to understand that early childhood is not only close to nature, but the entire human race is also a part of nature, just like any other life form. That is why children are inseparable from nature at this stage of life. Therefore, education at this stage of life should be "Education with nature."

This has a far-reaching consequence for the survival of all living beings coexisting with nature and preserving the environment and natural habitats of all life forms, including humans, for posterity. All living beings, including all animal and plant forms, are integral to the ecosystem.

Indian ancient concept of Gurukul education

A Gurukul or Gurukulam education system was prevalent in ancient India, dating to around 5000 BC, and the 'students' or 'disciples' lived near or with the guru or teachers.

This system imparted knowledge in a natural environment conducive to learning without any harmful impact on nature; rather, it will aid in conserving nature and the environment.

Based on the concept of the Gurukul education system, the following fifteen (15) steps can be fortified in the modern childhood education system.

1. The childhood education system should focus on imparting applied knowledge in every field of life.

2. The system should be designed to create a perfect and synergistic combination of academics and extracurricular activities.

3. There should be a component of teaching around mindfulness and spiritual awareness to make the students better and complete individuals.

4. The system should focus on the development of the physical health of children and learning skills with inspiration to find their passion and enhance their skills.

5. This system should encompass methods to help personality development, self-confidence, self-esteem, intellect, and the ability to think for one's self and improve upon their character during the progression of life through its various stages.

6. Exploiting the manifold importance of this system, the modern education system should be upgraded with the introduction of the principles of the gurukul concept, which will offer value-based learning for acquiring knowledge and wisdom.

7. The system will also explore the child's uniqueness, where learning revolves around that. This aspect of the education system will offer healthy competition among the students and immensely reduce stress levels amongst them.

8. There are challenges to using education to empower individuals to build their mental and physical health and free them from stress, anxiety, and depression.

9. The system will create a positive and strong bonding between the teachers and students.

10. The modern system based on the gurukul education system will create a secure and assured learning environment for the overall development of the children.

11. The system will greatly emphasize a psychological method of teaching by

designing the children's required mind maps. Thereby the system will greatly reduce the psychological barrier to competing among them. Rather, it will teach them to compete with themselves to raise their achievements.

12. The challenges in the modern education system on personality development, ethical training, or moral conscience development can be overcome by introducing a new system adopting the principles and philosophy behind the Gurukul education system for childhood.

13. The Gurukul education system continues to remain relevant even in modern times. Even in today's digital era, some of the major ways the gurukul system worked can be relevant such as its focus on holistic education. This system facilitates generations of wholesome development through value-based education.

14. The gurukul system can bring about the needed change from academic learning to amassing knowledge in a practical manner that will go a long way in the life of the

individual and the society.

15. It can also encourage a child to discover their passion and not restrict themselves to books but help them find their ways per the call of their heart and mind in life.

A new approach to education with nature

Love of nature's tendency to know about nature and natural phenomena are some of the inherent characteristics of childhood. This learning inquisitiveness of childhood should be capitalized for an effective and better teaching-learning approach.

In this regard, it can be referred to the "Scandinavian approaches like the 'Forest Schools' movement," which has already started to have an impact in North American Early Childhood Education (ECE) settings," as referred by Brianna Flavin in his article on "Four Emerging Trends in Early Childhood Education, published in 2020.

It is a great approach to bring nature and environment closer to the school and the children's life. This is not only an effort to impart education in natural settings but also a way forward to understanding nature and learning about the need for its conservation and judicious use without causing any harm to the environment.

This approach immensely contributes to understanding and appreciating nature, which is essential for development. The "children learn about natural environments, develop fine and gross motor skills, and build a connection to their local ecosystem."

The entire approach of educating about nature has a far-reaching consequence of producing dedicated human resources through learning and protecting nature, preserving the ecological balance, and developing resilience to the undesirable effect of climate change.

Even if there are no forest schools in many places due to the paucity of the required resources, the following four ways of teaching through nature can be adopted.

1. The teachers can put in some serious effort by incorporating natural elements into the classroom,

2. Dedicating time for outdoor exploration, excursion, activities in natural surroundings,

3. Practical involvement of the children in small gardens, plantations, small animal rearing, breeding, etc.

4. The children should be allowed and taught to play with nature.

This would help the teachers and parents to bring out the children's feelings and inner self for making an effort to shape their future life and habitable environment.

CHAPTER 14

Childhood psychology, Mindset and strategic approaches

"The best education does not happen at a desk, but rather engaged in everyday living-hands-on, exploring, in an active relationship with life."

~ Vince Gowman

The teaching-learning activities in formal education in childhood revolve around a fixed set of course structures and methodology for the delivery and transfer of knowledge.

The ability and adaptability to the system is the first and foremost challenge in a child's life.

The interaction between the mental makeup of the child and the environment to which they are exposed in the school builds their character.

The children, at this point, experience four sets of situations and are liable to suffer from confusion regarding adapting to the system and acquiring education, knowledge, and wisdom.

The four situations are:

1. The first situation is the atmosphere at home, with their parents and other family members. They try to make the child aware of the surroundings, materials, and components of life and nature in the easiest and simplest way.

2. The second situation is the family members trying to provide the child with knowledge about what they see and express their inquisitiveness on various activities and life processes to understand and practice what is needed.

3. The third is the formal approach in schools to learn by the child in a structured way using textbooks under the guidance of the teachers.

4. The fourth situation occurs when the child

tries to understand with their perspectives whatever they see through their own eyes.

The conflicts and confusions that emerge in the child's mind under these situations create a huge challenge for the child, which must be overcome and resolved.

Developing and realigning the mindset of the children

Parents can play a big role in helping their children develop a positive mindset that will support them through their early years and life and beyond.

There are two types of mindsets - Fixed and Growth mindsets. The attitudes to failure and why some children are more motivated than others to learn and understand that people can display either a 'fixed mindset' or a 'growth mindset.'

The two mindsets are not mutually exclusive and they can turn around any time in life. The child may have a growth mindset about some things (often, their natural strengths) and a fixed mindset about others (usually the things that man is not naturally good at).

Mindsets begin to show in children from age three.

Both natures of the child and nurture contribute to mindsets. Researchers studying mindset in children opined that it is very encouraging if the child wants to change the mindset from 'fixed' to 'growth.'

It is stated that mindsets can be developed and taught, which means one can change mindsets throughout their lifetime.

Ten (10) steps and ways to realign the mindset of children in terms of their psychological behaviours, attitudes, and social justice are

1. Teachers must take responsibility in their day-to-day engagements with children to meet the challenges,

2. Teachers and academic administrators should be ready to bring about reforms wherever needed.

3. Developing awareness about the deep-rooted implications of childhood education.

4. Parents and Societal guardians bring about greater opportunities for young ones.

5. Empowerment of children for enabling understanding and respect for all.

6. Teachers must be aware of the challenges faced by childhood education in the changing scenario of the modern and evolving society,

7. Teachers and parents must realize society's needs and be prepared to handle the challenges of fabricating a well-knit childhood life.

8. All stakeholders must understand and practice reform with vision and commitment.

9. Parents must be aware of the challenge for children's education in modern times vis-à-vis their duties and responsibilities.

10. The parents must be prepared to exert their power with eagerness for the welfare of their children adorably and justifiably to win their hearts.

CHAPTER 15

Challenges in Childhood Education at school

"Education is the key that unlocks the golden door to freedom."

~ George Washington Carver

During the stage of childhood primary education, some of the problems encountered are as mentioned below, which have been analysed and presented here for adaptation and practice.

Eight Stress Creating pressures that need to be addressed

There are a lot of stress-creating pressures during the early school days, which are as follows:

1. Regular and fixed time of attendance daily.

2. Pressure for good results all the time.

3. Do well in each subject, no matter the child's interest.

4. Participate in all activities, whether interested or not.

5. Nobody shows interest in identifying the child's interests and passions.

6. To be a 'good student' all the time.

7. Make friends and search for like-minded ones.

8. Encountering a completely new and different environment due to frequent changes in the school.

The expectations of the above challenges are sometimes beyond the child's reach.

The case of a child away from his native place faces challenges enlarged much beyond their resolution of the same.

Ten issues posing a challenge in childhood education

Some issues pose challenges to the children in their

learning process during their schooling, as listed below:

1. Difficulty in adjusting to the conditions and finding the schoolwork difficult.

2. Communication problems with the teachers.

3. Lack or loss of concentration due to weakness, health, and understanding issues.

4. Examination phobia and stress for preparation.

5. Getting mental harassment due to adverse behavior from classmates, schoolmates, or teachers and bullying.

6. Difficulty in building friendships and maintaining good relationships.

7. Difficulty in avoiding trouble shooters, and tagged as a "bad student."

8. I feel like "nobody understands me" and unsupported.

9. Problems at home with day-to-day life and activities, livelihood generation issues of parents, lack of support, work and study environment, and relationship with the

family members.

10. Psychological pressure contemplating disciplinary action or punishment due to no fault from the self.

The following four (4) measures can be taken to reframe the challenges

1. Teachers, school authorities, and parents should immediately identify the problems that pose challenges to the child and take remedial measures against the issues and challenges as soon as possible.

2. The students should also be taught and guided as to how to face and overcome such a situation and inspire and encourage them to build up strength for the future.

3. Children should be trained and empowered in school by the teachers and at home by the parents to make them capable of facing and handling any such challenges by the child.

4. The children should also be encouraged and supported in such a way that the child always feels that they are not alone.

The institution and society also need to support the child to face the situation and overcome the challenges.

The mental health of the child is always the priority

Expert says:

"Please remember that, although school is important, it is not worth sacrificing your mental health for. Your mental health always comes first. You do not need to be the best to be good enough." (Laura)

Identifying the problems at school that may affect the child's mental health status is of utmost importance.

Ten (10) important signs indicating that the child is struggling with some or the other problems in the school are:

1. When one finds everyday tasks difficult—for example, going to school regularly, getting ready in the morning, or having the company of friends.

2. The child starts feeling a loss of confidence or feeling down.

3. Feeling anxiety on the way to school, thinking about the day ahead.

4. Inattentive and lack of interest in sharing ideas in class,

5. Difficulty in talking with friends and taking the backstage.

6. Lack of interest and confidence in handling or performing any work.

7. Un mindfulness in any activities.

8. Lack of focus, interest, and motivation to do school or homework.

9. Get stressed, angry on frequent occasions, and inattentive at any work.

10. Not going to school, hiding the fact from the teachers and parents.

As in the early stages of schooling, the child is often unable to understand the challenges which are affecting their daily life; the teachers, parents, and seniors have a big role to play in the feelings of the child, and in such a situation they should extend their support and help using different approaches with love and care at school and home.

CHAPTER 16

Struggling at school, a big Challenge in childhood Education

"The struggle you're in today is developing the strength you need for tomorrow. Don't give up."

– Robert Tew

The child's brain is innocent. It believes in everything which they see and feel. That is why they are very easily hurt if something is not felt to their liking, as experienced in previous occasions. As a result, they suffer from dissatisfaction and try to change the situation to their liking. If they can do that immediately, they are happy, but if not, they struggle.

It is an instinct in a child to strive to achieve what

the child desire by trying to correct and tackle the situation in the face of difficulty.

When a child does that in any form of eventuality, it indicates that the child is a fighter and can be a changemaker in life.

The teachers and child educators must work on this aspect of the child to grow.

Eight (8) ways to overcome the challenges of struggling at school

- The child should be trained and practice concentrating and working hard. In this regard, time is not a factor; progress counts in achieving the result of hard work.

- The child should always talk and be encouraged to talk to some trusted friends or persons, teachers, or parents without any hesitation.

- The child should always be encouraged and helped to talk and discuss with the teacher or parents as soon as the problem is observed.

- The parents must help the child to talk with the school authority about the problems with which the child is struggling for remedy. The child can also be guided to talk to any seniors or trusted persons about the problems for guidance.

- The child should be encouraged to spend time and talk with the people with whom the child feels comfortable, like the favorite teacher, student friends, family members, relatives, or friends the child might have outside of school. They can support the child and remind them that people do value them.

- If the child has missed school for a long time, support their return to school by helping them to make up their mind. If a child has stopped attending school, the class teacher or Headmaster/Principal may work with the child and their family to support and help build confidence to return to school.

- Parents have a bigger responsibility to keep track of the activities of their children. They should always be alert to see if any behavioral or psychological changes occur with the child. Besides trying to pacify the condition of taking an interest in the child, the parents should also talk to the school authority, including the class teacher. They can help sort out the problems with some remedial measures they are acquainted with.

- Help from social media and professional bodies or societies through their write-ups or advice can also be taken to overcome the child's problems at school.

Socialization in education

Socialization is one of the most important components of early childhood education and communication skills. Children who participate in early childhood education programs and work on them improve their much-needed social skills. Children learn crucial skills like listening, sharing, and taking turns with others in a preschool setting through participation.

The initial struggle the child faces after joining the school is the act of socialization with fellow students, teachers, and staff. Although the child has a tender mind during early school days, the brain used to function as mature, and therefore while making friends in school, the child needs care and guidance.

Ten (10) approaches may be made to take care of the issues that are

1. The child must be taught and aware that one should socialize but not at the expense of happiness and peace of mind. The focus is to be on becoming happy and having freedom of mind.

2. The schools should have a support system to help the child whenever needed to relieve anxiety and stress.

3. Children should be taught while making friends, they should be careful about the other person's or child's mindset as their psychology and approach towards others may not be the same and liked by everybody.

4. Friendship grows only with like-minded persons who are often difficult to access and may be proved wrong in time, even if assessed. The child should be taught to be prepared to face the situation and make corrections after realizing the truth.

5. The child should also be taught to make friendships or relationships with the right person and in the right place. It is challenging and tough to ascertain during the initial stage; therefore, teachers and

parents should be very careful and take precautions before it is too late and damage is done.

6. The child should be taught about the act of adjustment in any eventuality which may arise on various occasions.

7. The child must be trained to understand that everything the child does should not harm them and the friends involved.

8. Dysfunctional friendships can ruin the school experience of the child. Therefore, the child should be ready to face the challenge and overcome the stress.

9. The child should be taught to build a strong mind and be brave to face any problems or situations, come what may. If the child could realize this, more than half of the issues would be gone.

10. No matter how alone the child might feel, there is always someone the child can talk to and someone who can help. Try to look for the child and find out.

Bullying: What it is and how to overcome

Bullying is a problem that is prevalent in almost all educational institutions and schools. Bullying is the behaviour and persistent act of a person or group who hurts or frightens someone smaller or less power full or weaker than them and forces that person to do something they do not want to do. In other words, bullying is a form of aggressive behaviour in which someone intentionally and repeatedly hurts another person mentally, emotionally, or physically.

Bullying is the use of force, hurtful teasing, or threat against another person, and abuse aggressively to dominate or intimidate continuously. Bullying can be done individually or by a group mobbing. Bullying in school is also referred to as "peer abuse."

The act of bullying has been classified as nonverbal, verbal, or physical behaviour. Bullying is also classified as individual and collective based on the perpetrators involved in the act. Physical, verbal, and relational bullying is prevalent from primary school and continues into later stages in an individual's life.

Physical bullying is any bullying that hurts someone's body or damages their possessions.

Verbal bullying is one of the most common types of bullying. This is done by speaking, using of abnormal voice, or some form of body language and does not involve any physical contact.

Bullying usually begins at this stage and includes any of the following:

- Calling by derogatory name or nicknaming.

- Spreading rumors or lies about someone.

- Threatening someone.

- Yelling at or talking to someone in a rude or unkind tone without any cause.

- Mocking someone's voice or style of speaking

- Laughing at someone

- Use of undesirable body language to provoke and torture someone

- Insulting and making fun of someone

Other acts considered bullying include racist and communal comments, religious bullying abusing one's beliefs or faith, sizeist bullying referring to one's body size, bullying focusing on being of the opposite sex, etc.

Cyberbullying is now becoming a common practice through the use of technology to harass, threaten, embarrass, or target another person. This includes bullying by using email, instant messaging, social media websites, text messages, and mobile phones. It is stated that Cyberbullying is more common in secondary school than in primary school.

Bullying is considered a menace in educational institutions, particularly in schools, with its far-reaching consequences. It uses to disturb the entire environment of the school and causes harm to the social relationship among the children.

Bullying can also take a severe turn in the affected child's mind, which may spoil their career and studies and even threaten their life.

Prevention of bullying:

Bullying is a social evil that must be prevented to build a healthy atmosphere in schools.

Ten (10) measures can be adopted against the act of bullying

1. Teachers play an important role in preventing bullying with appropriate

intervention at the right moments as they spend most of their time with the students.

2. In the school context, the administrators and teachers should set clear boundaries and communicate seriously with the instructions that bullying is unacceptable and will not be tolerated, and violators shall be punished.

3. School authority, teachers, and parents together can play an important role in child or adolescent situations in schools to check the menace of bullying through proper motivation.

4. In schools, the authority should train their teachers and staff to make them know how to respond to bullying so that the situation does not aggravate and can be brought under immediate control.

5. There should be clear instruction that if somebody physically hurts a child or verbally abuses or is bullying, the child should immediately report to the teacher or staff what is happening for action.

6. If bullying happens at school, the child should talk to the parents at home and the

teacher at school. Ignoring the act may not always work for its remedy.

7. If the bullying happens outside school or online, the child should talk to their parents, close relatives, or even their friends' parents for immediate interventions.

8. All educational institutions should have an Anti-Bullying Helpline office and online platform to help raise awareness about bullying and redress the grievance at any time.

9. As a parent, one of the most crucial things to be done is to ensure that the child knows what bullying is. They should begin by explaining what makes for meaningful friendships and what does not with their children.

10. Teaching anti-bullying coping skills to children, carers, and teachers is an effective long-term means of reducing bullying incidence rates and a valuable skill set for individuals.

Some have argued that bullying can teach life lessons and instil strength and opine that being a target of bullying can teach a child "how to manage disputes and boost their ability to interact with others,"

Creating anti-bullying mentality

It's very important to teach children in schools and parents to create an anti-bullying mentality.

Teaching the kids not to cause any disturbance or inconvenience to other children is simply one aspect of this.

Children need to understand that bullying is counterproductive and works against making friendships which is a critical requirement of human life. Teaching the kids about appropriate internet conduct is a must for eradicating cyberbullying.

Frame a Clearly Defined Code of Conduct to practice

Framing a set of guidelines or code of conduct for how employees and staff members of the school should be in place to be followed to prevent bullying of the children/students. A vigilance squad engagement may also be useful.

Bullying prevention help zones and helpline:

Bullying is the most common phenomenon in school. The children in the school must live with it by counter-challenging the challenges created by bullying. The kids in the school should be made known that they are not alone in fighting these challenges. Their teachers, Principals, parents, family members, and even the Samaritans are with them, and all of them can support the children to overcome the shock of bullying.

Handling Instances of Bullying

If a child report being bullied, one should first decide to meet with school staff face-to-face. This will make it easier for you to be ready if the situation worsens and other external sources need to get involved. Quick action against bullying is a must.

Read the signs as expressed by the child's behaviours

For many children who have been suffering from any struggle, constraints, and difficulties and/or are being bullied, their behaviours become conspicuous and they unknowingly emit signals that the parents and teachers must catch. They do not report it to anyone. Take notice of any indications suggesting the child has been suffering. Some of these signs include the following:

- Mood and personality of the child changes

- Struggling with school attendance and examination marks/grades

- Avoiding or neglecting favorite school activities

- Feeling unwell and having some health issues like stomachaches, headaches, and other illnesses

- Feeling depressed and not willing to talk.

Immediate action may be planned and taken in such a situation with appropriate strategies as required.

CHAPTER 17

Redrafting the Challenges: As faced by Teachers and Educators

"The greatest gifts you can give your children are the roots of responsibility and the wings of independence."

~ Denis Waitley

The following approaches are effective for redrafting the challenges faced by all concerned including the teachers, educators, and parents in imparting childhood education.

SWOC (Strength, Weakness, Opportunities, Challenges) analysis

The (SWOC) analysis in various studies indicates

that the teachers and students of early childhood and primary-level teaching face challenges and opportunities in their teaching process.

Every year the challenges may be of different types and magnitude as the situations differ and the psychology of the taught are also varied.

On the one hand, the teachers need to be resilient enough to the conditions while keeping their passion for guiding the students; on the other hand, the parents also need to play a pivotal role in supporting their wards' morale high and strong. However, at this point, their mental and psychological stress remains at different levels of absorption capacity and understanding due to their inherent and diverged family or social differences and inputs.

The students, the children of early childhood and primary level, must be molded to become resilient to any adversity and complexity of any situation. However, it is not an easy task to perform and achieve. Therefore, this needs to be done by a special type of person with the community's perfect and desired support system.

The educationists and the academic administrators

must be willing to invest in our future human resources by providing them with the required intellectual resources, infrastructure, and methodology for penetrating young minds and hearts to support the thought process of early childhood.

Empower the Children to face and overcome the challenge

The children should be aware of the bullying while admitted to the school and taught what bullying is all about and how to encounter or take remedies. When the child meets or sees the occurrence of bullying, it is crucial to teach them how and when to report it and explain why they should not ignore it.

The children should be provided with the resources and willpower to cope with bullying. One can also educate the child to practice walking away and avoiding any scuffle with anybody, silently approaching an adult, or firmly asking the bully to stop.

One should act quickly when the child is in distress or unhappy. Addressing bullying immediately when it occurs is the most effective method to stop it and its further recurrence. There is no point to wait till a situation has passed to discuss and act afterward.

Dealing with the emotional Health of a Child

It is the duty of the parents and teachers to increase the child's mental strength to keep the morale of the child all the time.

It is also the responsibility of the parents and teachers to make the child understand the motivational acts very clearly.

Twelve (12) such motivational acts to make the child feel strongly are

1. That you (every child) only know who you are, i.e., you as a human being.

2. Your inner self can be defined and created by you, not others.

3. You know your strength and never try to undermine it.

4. On every occasion, you rise and charge yourself full of your energy.

5. You never be afraid of fighting for the cause.

6. You always try to enrich yourself by acquiring knowledge and wisdom.

7. Be brave and rely on your capability and never have an iota of doubt about it.

8. Never bow down to any adverse condition, and never think that nothing is in your favour at any moment. Think that you can face the challenges to overcome.

9. Open your heart, and speak out to your near and dear ones. Letting it out will make you feel so much better.

10. Always be yourself and have full confidence, and you will flourish. Yes, but you may think it to be so hard right now, and you may think everything feels like it's against you, but it's not true; it's a misnomer. Never give a chance for this feeling to overpower you.

11. Be optimistic, hope for the best, and work hard. You will achieve.

12. Lastly, you must be able to see your worth and appreciate it so much more than you think. Being bullied or anything or any comment or remarks against you is scary,

painful, and hard to digest - but you don't have to suffer in silence. Speak to someone you trust to let them know what is happening, and together, you can work on and reverse the entire episode to improve it. Once you do this, winning will be your habit.

CHAPTER 18

Overcoming the Challenges for success in childhood education

"I don't run away from a challenge because I am afraid. Instead, I run toward it because the only way to escape fear is to trample it beneath your feet."

~ Nadia Comaneci

"Look for the good in every situation. Seek the valuable lesson in every setback. Look for the solution to every problem. Think and talk continually about your goal".

~Brian Tracy

Childhood is the first step of human life to make

itself aware of the surroundings and the environment to fit into the life process. Children are innocent and have no knowledge of anything good or bad and no idea about the adoption of anything. Slowly and carefully, they try to learn with experience to fill up their inner self with knowledge and skills through a process of their imagination. This process is enhanced through deliberate instructions, arguments, and assessment by their parents at home and the teachers at school.

Different stages of childhood can be constructed by adapting to various teaching methods and upbringing. There are three macro constructions of childhood. These are the tabula rasa child, the developing child, and the agency child. The tabula rasa construction of childhood assumes that children as 'empty' vessels that must be filled with knowledge and skills.

It is observed to be very pronounced in Asian countries, and the school learning process has been traditionally extended. The developing child construction is the period in the human life span when children naturally pass through universal and sequential stages of development.

The children of the latter stage can act deliberately, speak for themselves, and actively reflect on their social worlds, shaping their lives and the lives of others. In all these stages, education plays a significant role, reflecting the success of the methods and system of education.

It is desirable to have both formal and informal ways of teaching and training or in combination for knowledge transmission in early childhood.

Children generally face the teacher in front of the classroom, who is expected to impart the subject knowledge by explaining the 'lesson' as reproduced in the subject book. With the result, it becomes a theoretical exercise.

Usually, it is the general tendency of parents in developing countries to exert pressure on their children to get high marks in a formal 'test-loaded' pedagogy as their child's opportunity to excel depend on such results.

The Swiss psychologist Jean Piaget, the chief proponent of this construction whose work contributed to the understanding of Developmental Psychology vis-à-vis the growth of childhood education.

The construction of childhood is most evident in countries such as the UK and the US. It is embedded in the national guidelines for teachers in the early childhood education and care (ECEC) sector.

One consequence of this construction was the emergence of 'child-centred' and progressive education as early as the 1960s.

It is a fact that children's natural curiosity and the desire for understanding had to be given priority for learning through exposure to real-life situations, experiences, and activities.

The Early childhood education and care (ECEC)

As defined by UNESCO, Early childhood education and care (ECEC) is the "holistic development of a child's social, emotional, cognitive, and physical needs to build a solid and broad foundation for lifelong learning and wellbeing.

Seven (7) effective ways to overcome the challenges of preschool education are

1. Provide a safe and stimulating environment in which children can feel happy, secure, and compatible,

2. Encourage children to explore, appreciate, and care in respect of their environment,

3. Encourage emotional, social, physical, creative, and intellectual development and welfare of children,

4. Encourage positive attitudes to self and others and develop confidence and self-esteem,

5. Create opportunities for play for physical and mental exercise and well-being,

6. Provide opportunities to stimulate their interests, imaginations, and hobbies,

7. Extend children's abilities to communicate ideas and feelings in various ways and approaches.

Scientific Evidence-based ways and protocols in the Childhood Education system must be practiced. Intelligence is not a set genetic trait alone. It is a changeable, flexible ability to learn and stimulate the brain that can improve over time.

Ten (10) ways to follow childhood education needs are

1. The key is to practice lifestyle habits that support, protect and improve the brain and intelligence.

2. Two types of intelligence are (a) Crystallized intelligence, vocabulary, knowledge, and skills. Crystallized intelligence typically increases as the child gets older, and (b) Fluid intelligence, which makes intelligence provides the ability to reason and think abstractly.

3. Read on to learn what science has to say about the different ways the child can boost crystallized and fluid intelligence.

4. Reading helps boost intelligence. Childhood education should devote to the habit of happiness in reading. Reading stimulates every part of the brain and the neural connections between them.

5. Reading for empowering the brain for multiple cognitive functions, including attention, predicting working memory, long-term storage memory, abstract reasoning, comprehension, and visual processing of letters.

6. Reading enhances connectivity between regions of the brain involved with comprehension. This effect can last a couple of days after reading, suggesting long-term benefits for which the required time may be considered.

7. Getting sufficient sleep is essential for supporting optimal cognitive function created throughout the day by the brain to consolidate memories. This act enhances the ability of the brain to learn new information. Adequate sleep is important, and even mild sleep deprivation negatively influences memory.

8. Food and balanced nutrition are important for a child's brain development and function to carry on all the physical and mental activities. Therefore, the child should be given nutrient-rich food to boost brain health and support brain function. Food rich in Omega-3 fatty acids and Vitamin K plays a role in brain cell survival and cognitive performance.

9. Continuing learning habits and education is the key element to increasing intelligence. A

longer duration of education is linked to higher intelligence, and it is a lifetime process.

10. Continuing education also increases cognitive function, protects the brain, and adds to the learning process for developing more intelligence. Some examples of continuous learning and education are acquiring knowledge from any available sources of knowledge like reading newspapers, books, and magazines, listening and watching podcasts, watching TED talks, attending lectures or workshops, picking up a new hobby, learning a new language, read the information on new subjects, etc. Knowledge and intelligence are two different things. One can be educated by obtaining degrees or diplomas through formal studies and education, but knowledge and intelligence are beyond that.

A human being is a social animal or creature; that is why children should always be taught to be social. This helps in the enhancement of their mental makeup and fitness. Socialization stimulates the mind and cognitive ability of the child.

Sharpening the brain for Intelligence

Intelligence immediately strikes the brain to respond and stimulate the brain to solve problems and learn new things promptly. Intelligence is not about knowing more than other people. It's about stimulating one's brain by staying curious and alert.

One can boost the health of the brain and its efficiency and thereby enhance intelligence over time. It is not only one factor that one is also born with inherent intelligence. One should always keep on sharpening it through use and practice. Otherwise, it simply goes on decaying.

Eleven (11) effective ways to improve and sharpen intelligence

1. Like any other parts of the body, organs, and systems involved in everything for their functions, the child's brain also needs exercise for its normal functioning and to improve its activity and efficiency. Therefore, the brain also needs to be active and cared for all the time.

2. When the brain is active, the person remains

alert. Exercising the brain to improve memory, focus, or daily functionality is a top priority in children and grownups. This boosts memory power and provides deep concentration and focus, making the child respond instantly to different activities and tasks.

3. The child's brain should always be sharpened with some exercises or tasks to keep the child mentally alert.

4. Besides studying them at school and home, they should also keep on exercising their brains with extracurricular and cocurricular activities and hobbies of interest. There are many such activities like drawing, painting, dancing, playing indoor and outdoor games, adventuring something in nature, concentrating on new plantations in the garden, rearing some small animals, trying to find and walk down a route during holidays, solving puzzles, having a quiz, meditate and focusing in one's interests, etc. which dramatically improve the ability of the brain. Doing jigsaw puzzles involves multiple cognitive abilities and is a protective factor for visuospatial cognitive aging. Listening to

music, learning a new language, learning a new skill, and practicing vocabulary also can be great ways to challenge and exercise the brain.

5. Practicing a new skill and habit of building a strong and rich vocabulary contributes towards developing a stimulating brain. This can be achieved by frequent participation in different tasks and assignments.

6. Using all the senses together and performing several activities simultaneously in everyday life produces a big challenge to the brain and mind; always sharpening cognitive skills are some common brain exercises.

7. Learning and practicing adaptability in any adverse, uncommon, or new environment is another key component of intelligence. It describes one's ability to adjust to new or changing situations. This strength of adaption and adjustment capability of the brain brings the development of resilience and the ability to recover from adversity.

8. The child should be taught to keep trying until the required results are achieved;

bouncing back is another form of mental strength attained through rigorous attention, focus, and determination.

9. Focusing on brain power and health is one of the best things one can do to improve children's concentration, focus, memory, and mental agility.

10. Emotions are part of life. Emotions can understand life's values and provide the ability to develop intelligence to apply in recognizing and handling complex situations and exercising self-control to express feelings at appropriate times in safe and healthy ways.

11. Regulation and handling of emotion is a skill. It can be developed with practice and through strong interpersonal communication.

CHAPTER 19

The Challenges to the parents

"If parents want to give their children a gift, the best thing they can do is to teach their children to love challenges, be intrigued by mistakes, enjoy effort, and keep on learning."

~ Carol Dweck

The influence of the family, particularly the child's parent, plays a big role in developing the personality and character-building of the child. In the child's early life, the parents are the role model.

The child learns everything from their parents and is greatly influenced by their upbringing. The parents shape their child's early life philosophy.

The child explores their parents, their qualities, and their teachings. The parents should train their child to explore new things and try to expose the child to varied environments to gather experience and learn. The child will then resolve their curiosity and excitement of learning new things.

Making mistakes is natural. Mistakes are made by doing something only. It should be taken on a positive note. Everybody learns by making mistakes. The only thing is that they should not give up until the errors are corrected. The parents should make the child understand that something good and new things come out after attempting to correct the mistakes.

Parent's role in developing the identity and personality of the child

The children are known by their parents. However, their identity needs to be created by their parents. The parent's upbringing of the child, the teaching of good practices, morals and values of life, and respectful behaviours and living leads to building the child's character and identity.

Parents should always teach them the right things and approach the elderly and society. The influence of family life and the relationships among family members besides the parents greatly influence the child's character-building and personality development.

Duties of the Parents

Eleven (11) important duties of the parents while grooming the child and developing good quality traits in them are:

1. Parents must be role models for their children.

2. Understanding the child is the key to everything. The parents should give the child proper attention, time, and companionship.

3. To provide all support for the child's well-being- physically and mentally.

4. They should take the responsibility of teaching and guiding in every situation so that they can learn from their mistakes.

5. They should love their child and teach them to love and maintain a good relationship with all their friends, family members, neighbours, and others.

6. Parents should provide their children with the benefit of self-discipline and moral guidance.

7. Teach the child to experience a wide range of activities in social life.

8. The child should be taught to respect and help others.

9. They should be trained to be self-disciplined and to take responsibility.

10. The child should also be taught to be aware of their surroundings, the people around them, and the art of maintaining a good and cordial relationship with others.

11. Parents should always be helpful to their children, influence them, and be conscious of their eagerness to help others with their actions and behaviours.

Rendering the relevant and minimum services for young children before they start elementary school education is yet to take momentum in many countries. However, awareness of the value of early childhood education and care (ECEC) is growing. This awareness trend is gradually becoming popular in countries with economically poor backgrounds. Earlier, this social attitude was not so when the education of young children was regarded as the family's sole responsibility.

However, in any situation, the responsibilities of the parents are enormous. In most developing countries, the parents are not able to be fully involved due to work as well as economic pressure.

It is accepted that parents have to engage themselves with their children in helping them to grow and acquire knowledge and experience to become individually and socially competent to stand before any challenges for success and happiness.

Children learn much about their identity and subjectivity from their parents in the first few years of life. The foundations of their social attitudes and human values are subconsciously transmitted from parent to child. Therefore, parents should be aware of how they interact with their children at any time.

In many countries, reading and storytelling by parents to their children is a major activity in guiding the children towards building their character, understanding moral values, honesty, and developing kindness towards their kith and kin and others. Reading stories with children is another activity that is popular with many parents. However, the choice of stories is critical, and the parents should be incredibly careful so that the sensitive issues of social order and human behaviours do not get a chance to affect the mindset and imagination of the child adversely.

Social responsibility and obligations should be practiced in the family for the upbringing of the children.

CHAPTER 20

Encouraging and Inspiring for Positivity in Childhood Education

"Believe you can, and you are halfway there."

~ Theodore Roosevelt

The positivity of the parents and teachers is the most important aspect of grooming and educating the children. Therefore, they need to concentrate on these traits meticulously and see that the children benefit from these efforts.

Twenty (20) effective ways and approaches for inspiring and developing positivity while grooming and educating the children:

1. The child looks up to their parents and teachers, try to find their role models, and

learns from them. The child learns from the behaviour of their role models, which can encourage positive thinking, learn how to express their emotions, and be happy and mentally healthy. The child should be inspired only by positive stories. Showing something good on one's own is always better than only pieces of advice. Children are very sensitive to that. They want to see anything before they practice.

2. The child should always be encouraged to express their feelings by acknowledging and appreciating the child's feelings and emotions which helps them to develop a positive mindset.

3. The negative emotions and vices of the children should be taken care of, telling them that these are temporary phenomena and normal as human beings, and they should be taught to remove these, which will pass in due course of time. These should be handled with tolerance and practice.

4. The child should be taught to brainstorm to find potential solutions to their issues. This approach will empower the child to develop

a problem-solving attitude and mindset to look at things positively over time.

5. An effective review emphasizing the day's positive events will teach them to bring out their efforts for success. All negatives may justifiably be discarded and removed from their mind. This will build a strong mind to focus on the positive things in the future.

6. Hand holds the child to practice positivity to learn and recognize the positive aspects of life and to develop an optimistic attitude. Positive reflection is a must for any activity to feel satisfaction. This will lessen and remove stress throughout their lives.

7. The child should always be surrounded by positive-minded people and in an optimistic environment. The family and friends of the child should always try to create an impact on who surrounds them. They also have a large influence on the child's outlook on life.

8. The child should be taught to recite or sing a positive affirmation daily. Self-talk has a tremendous impact on the development of a strong mind. Empower the child with some scripted phrases to repeat and talk over time

to remove negative feelings or negativity of looking at things. For example, "if he/she can do this, why not I," "I can, I will," "this is not the end, I will overcome,"

9. Develop the habit of treating failures as learning opportunities in the child, and encourage the child to treat failure as a part of the road to success. Teach them to analyse failure and reconstruct the path to success by learning lessons from it. Negativity has no place in one's life.

10. Inspire the child to exercise the brain and to take the challenges of solving problems, teach the child to face and overcome the challenges and make them understand that it's a great experience and resolve. When the child fails, let them discuss the situation, review their mistakes, explore their strengths, and apply them to build a new strategy to overcome and do better next time.

11. Children should be taught to focus on their strengths and transform their weaknesses into opportunities. Once the child habitually focuses on their strength, they will gradually convert their weaknesses into opportunities and excel in life.

12. Explore the positive and strong attributes and bright areas of work where the child is active and interested. The child should be inspired and encouraged to help them shift their mindset to focus on their strengths in those areas. This will help build confidence in the child, and given the opportunity, they will gradually focus on the things they do well.

13. Always talk about the good and brighter side of the child, which will build confidence in them. Consequently, let them apply their effort with success, and they will be happy. Help the child to explore their domain and teach them to capitalize on that and excel.

14. Always remind the child and talk about the talents and qualities they have. This will encourage and inspire them to concentrate on these, and they will feel good. Provide the ways and opportunities and facilitate to inculcate their talents. Bring their attention to their positive and remarkable characteristics to make them feel good and inspire them to think positively and practice to attain the goal and achieve.

15. The child should be allowed to enjoy life and do what they love by discriminating against

what is good. The parent or teacher of the child has to be observed critically about the nature of the job the child is doing and the approach. If it is not a job having a positive outcome or character building, the child should be gradually taught to divert the attention to focus on the activity towards positivity. This should always be done with constructive criticism and guidance.

16. The classroom struggle should be removed as it creates stress and negatively affects the child, adversely affecting performance. This should be detected as early as possible and remedial measures should be taken to end the child's suffering. As the child at this stage lives in their dreamer phase, they should be allowed and helped to pursue their dreams and passions.

17. The children should be free to learn and grow at their own pace. But at the same time, guide them to develop their knowledge and skill.

18. Develop personalized curriculum to enhance the child's personality development and to pursue their dream and passion; the schools and teachers should make an effort to structure education towards that direction,

creating opportunities and options.

19. Making mistakes is an inseparable part of learning. Let them repeat until they make the correction and master a skill for themselves.

20. Inspire the child to raise their confidence level with a positive mindset by praising the child's all good quality traits. Allow them to speak out their feelings, listen to their viewpoints, and debate with constructive criticism.

Childhood can be shaped and constructed with positive vibes by these practices and principles, which are proven to be an essential part of the process of human development out of the child's life.

CHAPTER 21

Summary and Conclusions

Summary:

Childhood is the most sensitive and delicate phase of life. It is full of varied challenges, from mindset and character building to giving shape to the future life. At this phase, the children take their life easy and are not particularly concerned about their challenges.

Settling down with positive outcomes and achievements in this phase of life is very crucial. Childhood often encounters many challenges before starting the other phases of life. Therefore, their well-being and education need to be designed so that the children are empowered to face society's changing scenario and needs. In the process, the parents, teachers, educators, mentors, and motivators play a significant role in reframing the challenges for achieving success and happiness in their life.

In the past, childhood was more akin to nature and simplicity of understanding the world and relationships with their parents and society. Childhood's educational and learning environment is fast changing with the evolving socioeconomic and cultural transformations worldwide. The challenges present-day teachers and parents face in identifying the multifaceted problems concerning childhood teaching-learning systems are enormous. Evolving the required solutions for mitigating the issues, constructing road maps, and discharging the required action plans for implementation is also a daunting challenge faced by teachers, parents, and society.

Different societies have carefully discussed and framed early childhood education and care. Reform, transformation, and streamlining are possible, but it needs the understanding, commitment, and vision of those empowered to do it responsibly.

Teachers have considerable responsibility in their day-to-day engagements with children to perform. Attaining achievement passes through many constraints and challenges amidst the prevailing social attitudes and injustice. Therefore, parents and teachers need to become much more aware of the power they exert over their children to use their intelligent applications of educational principles in a more comprehensive, proactive, and democratic way to promote the mental growth of the children.

The mental journey of the child without affecting their mental health always comes first at school and home. Therefore, their emotional health needs greater attention in their education and nurturing. Various facets of understanding for mitigating the challenges faced during childhood have been described.

Elaborated and discussed the following essentialities to reframe and overcome the challenges of childhood mind and education:

1. Fifteen (15) qualities of the teachers of early education.

2. Ten (10) issues posing a challenge in childhood education and correction measures.

3. Ten (10) important signs indicate that the child is struggling with some other school

problems.

4. Eight (8) ways to overcome the challenges of struggling at school.

5. Ten (10) approaches to take care of the issues of socialization and friendships.

6. Ten (10) measures can be adopted against the act of bullying.

7. Ten (10) ways to follow the childhood education needs.

8. Eleven (11) effective ways to improve and sharpen intelligence.

9. Fifteen (15) steps for the fortification of the modern system of childhood education,

10. Seven (7) issues and approaches for effective modulation of childhood and nature,

11. Four (4) ways of teaching through nature for adoption in the system,

12. Ten (10) steps and ways to realign the mindset of children in terms of their psychological behaviours, attitudes, and social justice,

13. Eight (8) ways to overcome the challenges of struggling at school,

14. Ten (10) acts of socialization of the child.

15. Twelve (12) motivational measures to increase the child's mental strength to keep the morale high.

16. Ten (10) scientific evidence-based childhood education must be practiced in teaching-learning.

17. Eleven (11) duties of the parents to perform while grooming the child and developing good quality traits.

18. Twenty (20) approaches and codes for encouraging and inspiring positivity in child education.

This is done to facilitate and prepare the children for approaching other progressive phases of life till the adult stage, build their educational base and career, and attain satisfaction, fulfilment, and happiness.

Conclusions:

The challenges children face in physical, social, emotional, language, and cognitive development have been identified and explained. The impact of school and social circumstances on children's mental health has been analysed, and suggestions for identifying and addressing behavioural changes in children have been provided. Strategies for empowering children to overcome challenges and develop a positive mindset have also been discussed, focusing on the important role of schools, teachers, parents, and society in this process. Ways to improve children's intelligence and performance, and help them achieve a happy and fulfilled life, have also been outlined.

Acknowledged with thanks:

1. https://www.pinterest.com/pin/5-developmental-domains-of-early-childhood-development--644999977854264559/

2. https://extension.unl.edu/statewide/knox/growth-mindset-in-early-learners/

3. https://www.iamyello.com/role-of-a-teacher-in-early-childhood-education#:~:text=While%20teachers%20entertain%20children%20with,through%20a%20variety%20of%20methods.

4. https://www.prodigygame.com/main-en/blog/school-struggles/

5. https://www.cdc.gov/childrensmentalhealth/index.html

6. https://www.samarael.com/nbece

7. https://www.goshen.edu/merrylea/nature-based-early-childhood-education/

8. https://www.collegevaluesonline.com/challenges-facing-early-childhood-education-teachers/

9. https://www.intechopen.com/chapters/77529

10. https://www.educationcorner.com/motivating-your-child-to-learn.html

11. http://www.nurtureland.com.sg/how-to-help-students-develop-a-positive-attitude/

12. Eyal N. Danon (2020) "The Principle of 18: Getting the Most Out of Every Stage in Your Life."

13. Healy M. (2018) "The emotionally Healthy Child." Novato, CA: New World Library